IN LAHORE

a contemporary guide to the city

In Lahore: A Contemporary Guide to the City
Published 2016
inlahore.com

ISBN: 978-1-5272-0186-6
Copyright © Kelsey Hoppe 2016

Printed at Topical, Lahore
info@topicalprinters.com

"Jinnay Lahore nahi wekh-e-ya
aou jamiya nahi."

"If you've haven't seen Lahore
you haven't been born yet."

—Lahori saying

This book is dedicated to all the Pakistanis we know
some well and some only briefly
but all of whom made our stay in the country a joy.

You have all suffered through dark days
many of you have lost friends and family
This book is our small contribution to a new era
and a celebration of all that is and is to come.

Design

The colours in this book were derived from a single fresco
on the ceiling of an entryway in the Lahore Fort pictured here.

Author
Kelsey Hoppe

Pictures by
Ben French
Taimoor Baig
Kelsey Hoppe

'Lahore, Lahore hai' is all that is necessary.

Lahore is the centre for much of the arts, culture and intellectual thought that drives Pakistan. It has always been a centre of education, being home to the University of Punjab (one of the oldest universities in South Asia), Aitchison College and the National College of Arts. It boasts a publishing industry that produces approximately 80 percent of Pakistan's books and hosts several important mosques, churches, tombs, temples and shrines.

This rich amalgam that is Lahore makes for an immensely pleasurable visit, but provides some challenge when writing a city guide. To start with there has been no definitive historical literature produced on the city, and many of the websites and books which cover Lahore's past contradict each other on dates and places. Also, restaurants and shops come and go with alarming regularity so capturing them all is virtually impossible. Inevitably, the moment this is published it will be out of date and there will be no shortage of opinions and arguments about why *the* best restaurant or shop was left out. Hopefully, both Lahoris and visitors will forgive these shortcomings.

In creating this guide, we are indebted to the kindness of innumerable people who imparted their knowledge and fondness for the city. Taimoor Baig, whose pictures have helped us express the essence of Lahore.

Naheed Bilgrami and Fakir Aijazuddin who generously edited this edition. And, Babar Ali—a Lahori institution himself—who gifted us books, knowledge and his infectious love of Lahore.

There are several authors whose brilliant books about Lahore we relied heavily on as they shone light on different aspects of the city and are quoted here. First, *The Illustrated Beloved City* by Bapsi Sidhwa. If anyone wishes to fall in love with Lahore this collection of essays and recollections is a good place to start. Next is Anna Suvorova's *Lahore: Topophilia of Space and Place*, which gives a far more in-depth and academic perspective on Lahore. Then, *Lahore The Architectural Heritage* written by Lucy Peck with the Babar Ali Foundation. Anyone interested in the history of Lahore would do well to pick this up as it includes several walking routes through the Old City that are worth following.

As with travel in most places, people find in Lahore what they are prepared to see. Unfortunately, Pakistan's reputation has been sullied over the past twenty years. If a visitor's preconceived notion is that Lahore is a dangerous, unfriendly, poor, dirty, smelly and chaotic city this is undoubtedly what they will find. However, anyone who visits Lahore with an open mind and the slightest sense of adventure will instantly be taken in by its romantic charm and unfailing hospitality. We hope this guide gives you a sense of these.

Useful Websites

A collection of helpful websites for those visiting or interested in Lahore.

Lahore City History: *lahore.city-history.com*

Lahore Nama – Searching for the city that was and ought to be: *lahorenama.wordpress.com*

Siddy Says – Fashion & Lifestyle blog: *siddysays.com*

Daastan-e-Pak – Bringing you the lighter, better, brighter side of Pakistan: *dastaanepak.com*

MangoBaaz – Information & Entertainment: *mangobaaz.com*

Humans of Pakistan – Telling Pakistan's stories one human at a time: *facebook.com/HofPak*

OCCO Lahore Architour: *facebook.com/OccosLahoreArchitour*

Country Roads Pakistan – Travel photography and essays through Pakistan: *facebook.com/Country-Roads-Pakistan-117140575301298*

Travel Across Pakistan (TAP) – Pakistani Travel & Lifesytle Magazine *destinations.com.pk*

Old Lahore Walkabouts – Beautiful pictures and video of Lahore from a bygone era: *facebook.com/OldLahoreWalkabouts*

Lahore, City of Gardens: *web.facebook.com/lahore.gardens/?_rdr*

Lahore City History: *lahore.city-history.com*

The Walled City Authority: *itdhub.net/wcla*

The Desi Tour Project: *desitourproject.com*

Pakistan Tourism Development Corporation: *tourism.gov.pk*

Youlin Magazine a cultural journal covering Pakistan and China. *youlinmagazine.com/upcoming-events-in-lahore*

Lahore Literary Festival: *lahorelitfest.com*

Lahore Music Meet: *lahoremusicmeet.com*

ArtNow Pakistan: *artnowpakistan.com*

All eventsLahore: *allevents.in/lahore*

Happening PK: *happening.pk/lahore*

Danka: *danka.pk*

My Art World: *facebook.com/myartworldgallery*

Lahore on Trip Advisor: *tripadvisor.com/Tourism-g295413-Lahore_Punjab_Province-Vacations.html*

Express Tribune, Lahore: *tribune.com.pk/lahore*

Dawn Newspaper, Lahore: *dawn.com/newspaper/lahore*

Lahore Conservation Society: *lcs.org.pk*

ABOUT LAHORE

Discover Lahore today

> "Lahore is a love affair,
> it has nothing to do with reason"
> – from Chowk.com

Lahore is the capital city of Pakistan's Punjab province, and considered the cultural heart of the country. It is the second largest city in Pakistan after Karachi, which is in Sindh province. Lahore is home to the largest native Punjabi population in the world and Punjabi is the primary language spoken. Urdu and English are also spoken but usually by those who have finished school. Lahore's population in 1998—the last time a census was conducted—was 6.5 million but it is now believed to have between seven and ten million people, making it roughly the same size as Cairo, London, Bangkok or New York.

The presence of the river Ravi is likely the reason a city developed here. The river then flowed by the walls of the Old City, but its course has shifted. It now flows to the northwest of the city, dividing the Indus plain from the land of the Ganges. All of Lahore sits southeast of the river, and has administrative divides separating it into nine 'towns' and 53 union councils. The rapid spread of the city doubled its geographic size in the last ten to fifteen years. Some of this spread has been according to city planning but much of it was unplanned. This can make Lahore crowded and chaotic in certain places and quiet and relaxed in others.

Fakir Aijazuddin describes Lahore as:

"...a federation of neighbourhoods, markets and special districts, each with a highly individual character. Functionally as well as architecturally, these neighbourhoods reflect consecutive historical stages of the city's growth."

Given that there are few high rise buildings, this collection of different areas, suburbs and neighbourhoods lends to the feeling that there is no real 'downtown' or centre. Rather, there are many centres—each with its own nature and purpose.

A newcomer to Lahore will not recognise when they are passing from one distinct neighbourhood to the next, but locals know the different areas well. The only exception to this is the Cantonment (Cantt) which is administered by the army so there are checkpoints at all entry and exit points. (Check your passport entry stamp as it might be stamped 'no entry' to the Cantonment. If this is the case you will not be permitted to pass through or visit the Cantt). It is not possible to give a description of every Lahore neighbourhood and in any case, as a visitor, there are only a few that are likely to be frequented. These are described on the following pages.

The Old (Walled) City

This area is described in detail in What to See page 50.

The Old City used to be *the* city of Lahore and all later areas and neighbourhoods spread out from it. Though there are few places to stay in or near the Old City, this is where you may end up spending much of your time as a visitor as many historic attractions are concentrated here. In the Old City you will also find the excellent Food Street, a stretch of food stalls and restaurants in what was once Lahore's red light district. Many of the restaurants are in restored traditional buildings (havelis) overlooking the Badshahi mosque.

Anarkali

Just to the southwest of the Old City is Anarkali. (See page 69 for more about the legend of Anarkali.) Anarkali was the first area settled outside the Old City – mainly by the British, who feared the dark, closed-in spaces and potential spread of disease in the Old City. The British first set up their Cantonment in Anarkali before moving it further southeast to Mian Mir where it sits today. The area grew rapidly in the early 20th century with Mall Road being built to connect Anarkali with the Cantonment. Anarkali is best known for its market which sprawls from the Lahori Gate of the Old City about a mile to the south. The market is made up of several bazaars where you can buy everything from medicine to cloth, jewellery and shoes.

Gulberg

Gulberg has the reputation of being one of the 'posh' areas of Lahore and a central business area. Homes here tend to be big and luxurious, and the entire area is sprinkled with shopping centres and restaurants. There are two large shopping markets—Liberty Market and Main Market—and along M.M. Alam Road there are many upscale shops and restaurants. Sporting and outdoor activities can be found at the polo grounds in Jilani Park, Qadaffi Cricket Stadium and the Gymkhana and Palm Golf Courses.

Defence Housing Authority (DHA)

DHA is an ever-expanding housing society that was originally built to provide housing for military personnel. It opened in 1975 and is very ordered with construction occurring in different phases and alphabetic blocks. Both military and civilian personnel live here now, and it is considered a very nice suburb. Part of DHA falls within the Cantonment (Cantt) but much of it does not. 'Y' and 'H' blocks are known for their shopping venues and restaurants.

The Cantonment

Simply called 'Cantt', this is considered one of the greenest, and 'leafiest' parts of Lahore and the housing is sought after. Some good shopping is found in Cantt, including Fortress Stadium, the Mall of Lahore and Hyperstar. The quickest way between the hotels/centre of Lahore and the airport is through Cantt. Sadly, however, 'Cantt' (Can't) is an apt description for foreigners. At all entry points foreigners are required to register their passports and can be denied access if they are not carrying it with them or if those on the checkpoints simply decide they are not allowed.

Model Town

Model Town was initially conceptualised by Khem Chand, a lawyer who wanted to build a new cooperative society for people of different religions and professions in Lahore. At the time of its inception, Model Town was three miles from the Lahore city boundary. The entire town was planned at the outset with schools, hospitals, parks and room for lawns and gardens with each plot. Electricity was provided by the town's own plant and the town had its own public transport system to take people to Lahore. Today, Model Town is entirely incorporated into the city of Lahore and considered a nice neighbourhood in which to live.

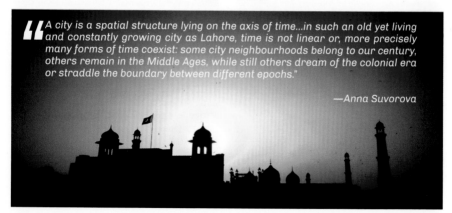

A city is a spatial structure lying on the axis of time...in such an old yet living and constantly growing city as Lahore, time is not linear or, more precisely many forms of time coexist: some city neighbourhoods belong to our century, others remain in the Middle Ages, while still others dream of the colonial era or straddle the boundary between different epochs."

—Anna Suvorova

The Red Light District (Heera Mandi)

Heera Mandi (Tibbi) is reportedly named after Hira Singh, the son of a nobleman during Ranjit Singh's rule, who was fond of women, dancing, and singing. Located near the new food street that faces Lahore Fort and Badshahi Mosque, Heera Mandi (which translates as diamond market) was once home to professional singers, dancers, and musicians who practiced traditional and classical arts. Alternatively called dancing girls, prostitutes, courtesans, nautch girls and tawaif, no one phrase is adequate to describe the women of the Heera Mandi mohalla (community) of the Old City.

During the Mughal and Sikh periods these cultured courtesans who danced, sang and recited poetry were considered talented artists, and patronised by men of wealth and social standing. They fell from favour during the British period being labelled prostitutes. During the 1950's they were given the official status of 'artists' but favour again shifted during Zia Ul Haq's military rule from 1978 to 1988 and their practices forbidden. Since that time, many of the women of Heera Mandi who could afford to have moved from the Old City. Those who remain continue with the traditional practices, but they are generally treated poorly and their work largely considered immoral.

One of the best known locations in Heera Mandi is the restaurant, Cucoo's Den. Its owner, Iqbal Hussain, was the son of one of the women who worked and lived there. He attended the National College of Arts and has become a leading artist in Pakistan and internationally. His artwork, portraying the lives of women in the mohalla, can be viewed on the first floor of the restaurant.

In 2005, Louise Brown, an anthropologist, lived in the mohalla and wrote an excellent book on the subject called 'The Dancing Girls of Lahore'.

A BRIEF HISTORY
Delve into Lahore's ancient past

Given its strategic location between Central and South Asia, it is easy to see how Lahore was central to much of the region's history for at least a thousand years. Some historians believe that a civilisation has been present on the site for as long as 4,000 years but the origins of the city are vague.

The legend of the city's origins is that it was founded by Prince Loh, the son of the Hindu god Rama, and that the name comes from the phrase 'Loh awar' meaning 'fort of Loh'. It is claimed that Alexander the Great passed through the city, but there is no written evidence of this. Around AD 150, the Greek astronomer and geographer Ptolemy wrote a book called *Geographia* in which he mentions a city called Labokala, which could have been Lahore. However, the most conclusive evidence of the city's presence is from the *Hudud al-'Alam* (*Regions of the World*) written in 982, which is held today in the British Museum. In it, Lahore is described as a town that is home to temples, markets and orchards.

To read through a history of Lahore's rulers is to understand much of the successive history of kingdoms, empires and seats of governments in Asia. Lahore has been conquered, plundered, and ruled by a virtually endless number of dynasties and people.

To begin only in the 600's AD, Lahore was ruled by the Rajputs who possessed an area from modern-day Multan to Rawalpindi. It was during, and immediately after, their rule that the reach of Islam extended into Pakistan with Hindu and Buddhist religions waning. Rajput rule ended in the 1100's when Lahore was sacked by Mahmud of Ghazni. The conqueror installed his Georgian general, ex-slave and reputed lover Malik Ayaz as governor of Lahore. Malik Ayaz rebuilt the city, which prospered under his rule. Ayaz's tomb can still be found in the Old City not far from the Rang Mahal shopping area.

After the fall of the Ghaznavid empire, Lahore was ruled by a succession of Muslim rulers called the Delhi Sultanate. But its architectural and cultural glory days were achieved under the reign of the Mughals.

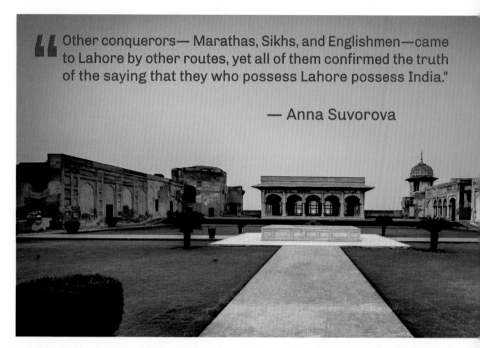

> **❝** Other conquerors— Marathas, Sikhs, and Englishmen—came to Lahore by other routes, yet all of them confirmed the truth of the saying that they who possess Lahore possess India."
>
> — Anna Suvorova

The Mughals, relatives of the infamous Genghis Khan, arrived in the 1520's from modern-day Central Asia and Afghanistan. During their near three hundred years' rule they built most of the historic sites for which Lahore is now known – including much of Lahore Fort, the Shalimar Gardens and Badshahi Mosque.

By the mid-1700's Mughal rule was waning and Lahore was occupied by different dynasties including the Durrani and Maratha. The Sikhs eventually captured Lahore and it became, once again, the capital of an Empire. Maharaja Ranjit Singh rebuilt the city and had a moat dug around it. By the mid-1800's the British controlled much of what is now India but the Sikhs had kept them at bay. After Singh's death, however, the Anglo-Sikh wars resulted in the British gaining control of Lahore.

British rule would last from 1849 to 1947. During this time, they 'invented' Urdu as the national language and expanded Lahore out of the Old City. Tearing down the city walls, they built their Cantonment several miles away in Mian Mir and constructed Mall Road to connect it to the Old City. The colonial style in which they built reflected European styles of the day.

Lahore played a special role in the independence movements of India and Pakistan. The 1929 Indian National Congress session was held at Lahore and it was during this meeting that the 'Declaration of Independence' was passed unanimously. Many great thinkers and political activists were detained by the British in Lahore's prisons. In 1940, the All India Muslim League (which would become the Pakistan Muslim League) met at a critical session in Lahore to demand the creation of the Pakistan state as a separate homeland for India's Muslims. Muhammad Ali Jinnah, its leader, publicly proposed the Two-Nation Theory for the first time.

Lahore suffered greatly at India's independence and the partition of Punjab. (See page 24 on partition) Punjab was sliced in two with one-third becoming an Indian state and two-thirds becoming a Pakistani province with Lahore as the new capital. Almost immediately, large scale riots broke out with Hindus and Sikhs being massacred by Muslims, and Muslims massacred by Hindus and Sikhs on both sides of the new border. In Lahore, thousands of people died and there was unprecedented damage to historic buildings. Some of the gates of the Old City were pulled down during this time.

Lahore was able to rebuild but the ethnic and religious diversity of the city was irretrievably altered.

In 1965, Lahore was once again the site of conflict as Pakistan went to war with India. This war concentrated along the border in the Wagah area near Lahore and trenches and bunkers used can still be viewed today. The war was settled inconclusively with both sides claiming victory.

From 1970 to the present Lahore has expanded in both population and geographic size becoming an industrial and commercial centre. Much of the modern construction in the city reflects these different decades.

A Small Note on "India"

"But I thought Rudyard Kipling lived in India..." Yes, Rudyard Kipling was born in what is now India but actually spent much of his time in the subcontinent in Pakistan. 'India' is a historically fluid term. Prior to the British occupation of the Indian sub-continent there was no 'India' or 'Pakistan'. The term India originally referred to the Indus river which flows through Tibet, Pakistan, and India. The entire area occupied by the British Raj (rule) came to termed India from 1858 to 1947. This means prior to 1947, any writing about 'India' could be referring to areas in modern-day India as well as areas in Pakistan, Nepal, Bangladesh or even parts of Burma.

Partition

"After this visit to my beloved Lahore, I realized that the politics of the two countries has practically nothing to do with the people who would love to meet those across the border, bound together as they are by a common language, culture and history. It is the Punjabis on both sides who suffered the most and paid the heaviest price at the time of the British withdrawal from the subcontinent...I recall a press report about a poster carried by someone from the Pakistani side which said, 'Akhiyan di lali dasdi hei, roye tusee wi ho, roye asi wi han' (Our red eyes reveal that you have wept and so have we)."
—Pran Nevile

In June 1947 the British agreed the 'Mountbatten Plan', which would grant India its independence from the British Empire two months later. As part of this plan, East (what is now Bangladesh) and West Pakistan would be 'partitioned' from India and be established as a new country. This was the outcome of the 'two-nation' theory that suggested that Hindus and Muslims were two separate nations because of their differing religious identities, and it would be impossible for them to live together under one state.

There are two 'independence' days as the British Viceroy of India, Louis Mountbatten, wanted to be at both events. Hence, the independence of the two new countries fell within minutes of each other on August 14th in Pakistan and the 15th in India. The two halves of Pakistan lay separated by India. It was not an auspicious start.

Immediately prior to, and following, Partition, Hindu and Muslim extremist groups throughout the Indian subcontinent had stirred up tensions, and the communal violence that followed resulted in the deaths of between 200,000–500,000 people. Approximately 14 million people were displaced as Hindus and Sikhs fled Pakistan and Muslims fled India. Many on each side of the border lost homes and businesses that had been in their families for generations. Many who fled never returned, even though they might still have family and friends on the other side of the border.

Cities like Lahore were previously multi-ethnic and multi-religious, but Partition changed that. While pre-partition Muslims had formed a majority of the population in Lahore, much of the land and business was owned by Hindus or Sikhs. Massacres, and rumours of massacres, of Muslims fueled more violence and massacres in and around Lahore against the Hindu and Sikh minorities

Some very good literature and films have been produced on Partition and the traumatising effect it had on both countries. In the movie *Jinnah*, Muhammad Ali Jinnah is called to account in heaven for the creation of Pakistan and the resulting violence. Books on Partition include Bapsi Sidhwa's *Ice-Candy Man* (now called *Cracking India*), *Freedom at Midnight* by Larry Collins and Dominique Lapierre, *A Bend in the Ganges* by Manohar Malgonkar, and *Midnight's Children* by Salman Rushdie.

Reunion

In 2013, Google produced an advertisement called *Reunion*, telling the story of two friends separated by partition. An older, now-Indian man, named Baldev, recollects his childhood youth in Lahore with his granddaughter. He, and his best friend, Yusuf, now Pakistani, used to fly kites and steal sweets from Yusuf's family's sweet shop. Baldev's family had to flee during partition and the commercial shows their grandchildren's efforts to reunite them. The commercial has been viewed on YouTube nearly 13 million times and the subtitles can be changed into nine languages. To view, google "reunion advertisement" and watch it on Youtube.

"My beloved city of Lahore
still standing not far from Delhi,
within quicker reach by air or train,
suddenly became a forbidden land
guarded by a sovereign state
of new ideologies, loves and hates.
Homes were lost and hearts were bruised
In both unhappy parts of Punjab."

– 'Spirit's Musings' by Prem Kirpal
quoted in Lahore: A Sentimental Journey by Pran Nevile

NEED TO KNOW

Plan a great visit

Currency & Getting Money

The currency in Lahore and, indeed the rest of Pakistan, is the Pakistani rupee (PKR). It has remained stable for many years now, hovering around 100 PKR to $1 USD. The notes most used are 10, 20, 100, 500, 1,000, and 5,000. There are also coins of 1, 2, and 5 denominations. While bank cards and credit cards can be used in certain locations (upscale restaurants and shops), cash is the most used form of transaction. Money-changing outlets are numerous but most people prefer to simply withdraw cash at ATM (bank machines). Bank cards should preferably be Visa, as only Standard Charter Bank will give cash for cards that are Mastercard. The fees for global transactions are usually charged by both the person's home bank as well as the bank in Pakistan and can be around $6 USD per transaction.

Prices & Tipping

Everything will need to be paid in Pakistani rupees as no foreign currency is accepted. Credit/bank cards are not widely used unless you are making a major purchase and even then you should check with the store first. Your bank will also likely block purchases made in Pakistan almost immediately if they haven't been informed that you are travelling here. To avoid this inform your bank before travelling.

In most shopping malls and many stores the prices will be marked. This means they are not negotiable and you should not bargain or try to negotiate the prices with the store staff. In open air markets and smaller stores where the prices are not marked it is assumed that you will barter with the store/ stall owner. There is no set formula for bargaining, however, and, unlike in other countries, the storekeeper will let you walk away rather than lower their prices.

Tipping is expected and encouraged for almost everything. Given the issues with unemployment and surplus of labour there are a lot of people to help you. Each of them will need to be tipped. This includes anyone who provides a small service for you by pumping your gas, washing your car windows, valet parking your car, guarding your car, or carrying your groceries. Tips for nominal services should range between 50-100 rupees. In restaurants, tips between 10%-15% are normal.

Electricity

The voltage is 220-240 volts and the plugs are European (two round prongs) or, in some places, British. Most appliances (including mobile phones and laptops) that have a multi-voltage adaptor need only a plug adaptor. High voltage items (such as kitchen appliances, hair dryers, etc.) will need either a voltage converter or a transformer. Plug adaptors, appliances and electrical items are relatively cheap in Lahore so if you intend to stay, or visit regularly, it is worthwhile to buy them here.

Communications

Pakistan is a well-connected country in terms of telecommunications. In Lahore, there are several mobile service providers and good coverage. There is 3G and, in places, 4G internet. That said, for a short-term visit it's a bit difficult to get a SIM for your phone. This is due to anti-terrorism efforts by the Pakistan Telecommunications Authority (PTA) which require every SIM to be linked with bio data to the user. For Pakistanis with an identification card (CNIC) this is no problem but it is not so easy if you're a foreigner. If you are here with an organisation on a longer-term visa, the organisation should get one for you. Be prepared, however, when your visa expires so will your SIM. If you are on a tourist visa, or a short-term visit visa, you need to go in person with your passport and valid visa to be registered at the mobile phone store. Again, the SIM will expire when the visa does. That said, WiFi is plentiful around the city so you can connect with communications apps like Skype and WhatsApp whenever you need to by stopping by at a coffee shop or hotel.

News / Newspapers

Before you come to Lahore, or while here, you might want to get information on the city that you won't find popping up in your normal newsfeeds. There are several English language newspapers published daily and all of them have websites. There are also a couple of weekly English papers which are widely read including: The Friday Times (thefridaytimes.com/tft) and Newsweek— Pakistan Edition (newsweekpakistan.com)

◆ The Express Tribune (tribune.com.pk)

◆ The News International (thenews.com.pk) publishes daily and has a city news section on Lahore (thenews.com.pk/print/category/lahore).

◆ The Nation (nation.com.pk)

◆ The Dawn (dawn.com)

Weather

Lahore has a temperate climate with the exception of the summer months (May-September) which are so hot that the entire population cocoons in a comatose, indoor, hibernation under fans and air conditioning. Those who can afford to, often spend several months abroad between April and August. Winter months are December, January, and February but the term 'winter' is relative. The coldest temperature ever recorded in Lahore was −1 °C (30 °F), which occurred in 1967. From late December to early February the city can also experience dense fog which makes driving difficult and can close the airports and motorway. Airlines will often shift their normal schedules to accommodate the fog. This is followed by spring which are the months of March and April. The summer months and monsoon months coincide in May, June, July, and August. During these months the weather is hot and humid, regularly reaching 40-45 °C (104 °F). The highest temperature ever recorded was 55 °C (131 °F) in 2007. The monsoon rains normally start at the end of June, and in July there is heavy rainfall and thunderstorms.

If you are planning a visit to Lahore, the months of February-April, or October-December are best.

Health

It is best to check with your embassy's, or home country's, health advice related to vaccinations and health precautions to be taken in Pakistan. It is likely that several vaccinations will be recommended. Polio is still endemic in Pakistan and the government and health department require an annual booster. You could be asked to produce evidence of this at the airport. Dengue is also another health concern, and mosquitoes in the summer months can be a nuisance. Mosquito repellent and room sprays are easily available in Pakistan, but if you're on a short visit it is easiest to just bring some with you. While tap water is available and is fine for bathing only bottled water should be drunk. Pakistan's stomach bugs are infamous for causing inconvenience to visitors so be cautious eating street food, or fresh vegetables.

Having travel insurance is always a good precaution and if you become ill while travelling call their emergency number for doctor and hospital recommendations. If you need to get to a hospital quickly however, try either of the below which will see walk-in emergency cases:

- ◆ Shaukat Memorial Hospital Cancer Hospital (shaukatkhanum.org.pk)
- ◆ Doctor's Hospital Outpatient Department (doctorshospital.com.pk)

Security

Emergency services are available by calling: 1122 (rescue.gov.pk)

Unfortunately, Pakistan has gained a reputation of being an extremely dangerous place. Like any country, there are certainly places in Pakistan which are very dangerous and it is inadvisable to go. Lahore is not one of them. Lahore has sadly experienced its fair share of terrorism but it is certainly not an everyday occurrence and while it is impossible to predict if, or when, an attack might happen most visitors to the city come and go completely unaffected by any terrorist-related event.

From a visitor's perspective, one of the positives of so few people visiting Pakistan is that Lahore is relatively free from beggars and touts. Rarely will you be approached by shysters attempting to sell you something or divert you. If someone at a historical site is offering a tour, map, or book a polite 'no, thank you' and continuing to walk is all it takes to continue on your way.

If you are a foreigner you will also be watched, or stared at, constantly and this can make some people uncomfortable. There is no reason to be paranoid, however, as this is usually done by people who have little contact with foreigners and are simply curious. Mostly, the ogling is done by men who are fascinated by a foreign woman, or by 'free boys' or 'free girls' who are groups (usually teenagers) with free time on their hands. If you are approached you will find that they're simply curious about what you're doing, where you're going and what you're buying. They might want to try out their English, ask you where you're from, why you're here, and what you think about Pakistan. They will ask for you to pose in pictures with them. Think of it as being a minor celebrity. You have two choices. You can either politely say no and keep going. Or, you can allow your picture to be taken and engage in short conversation. It's up to you, but remember that you're likely to have many of these requests while you're out and about. If you are uncomfortable you can tell them to stop by holding up your hand and saying, 'bas' which means, 'enough' or 'stop'. In most cases there is absolutely no harm intended. However, if you feel that someone is watching you in a more hostile manner, following you, or making you uncomfortable, then leave and tell someone. Also, it isn't culturally appropriate for a Pakistani man to approach, touch, or talk to women, so if you are a woman on your own ignore the approach, do not make eye contact and keep going.

While it is always good to be on guard and observant in a new place, the vast majority of Pakistanis are helpful, considerate, hospitable, and delighted you are here. They will want you to have a favourable view of their country so will go out of their way to assist you.

Lahore is a large city and, as in any big city, there are certain precautions which you should take to protect yourself from crime and accidents. If you are a foreigner, you will stand out from the general population and it will be assumed you are wealthy and Western. This can make you a target for certain types of crime—such as pick-pocketing and robbery. While it is unlikely that you will be a victim of crime or terrorism in Lahore, it is recommended that you read your country's travel advice and follow a few precautions so that you minimise the possibility of problems and enjoy your stay. A few general tips are below:

- ◆ Do not carry your passport or any other critical documents (driver's license, etc.) with you unless you know you need it. Carry a copy if you feel you need to have it with you.
- ◆ Do carry a form of picture identification.
- ◆ Do not wear expensive jewellery if you are going to be out on the streets or visiting historical sites.
- ◆ Do not use an expensive smart phone in public.
- ◆ Do not carry your credit/bank cards unless you intend to use them.
- ◆ Do not carry more than the equivalent of $100-$200 USD of cash in PKR on you.
- ◆ Be aware of your personal possessions. Do not hang a purse/jacket over a chair if it contains valuables.
- ◆ Do not give money to beggars. Simply smile, shake your head no, and keep going.
- ◆ When in the car, keep the doors locked and windows rolled up most of the way.
- ◆ Limit walking done outside at night and always with someone who knows the city.
- ◆ If you feel threatened while in public, go quickly to a brightly lit shop, market, or police station.
- ◆ Vary your movements. Don't leave and come back at the same time each day, even if you are staying for a short period of time.
- ◆ Almost all crimes in Pakistan begin with 'hostile surveillance' this means that someone watches you and what you're doing before deciding to commit a crime. While, as a foreigner you will attract a lot of attention, in Lahore, if you feel that you are being watched intently or you have a sense of unease in any place/situation then leave and come home or to another place of safety.
- ◆ Women should take a scarf with them when outside and use it as a head covering if necessary.
- ◆ Women should wear long sleeved, loose fitting clothes and men should wear trousers in public.

What to Wear

Influenced by Hollywood's portrayal of Pakistan as a backwater full of Islamic extremists many people labour under the misconception that they need to radically change their wardrobe when visiting the country. You can delay your burqa shopping as western dress is quite the norm in Lahore. While it is advisable for women to cover their arms and legs this can usually be easily done without buying a new wardrobe. For women, loose-fitting clothing is better, especially if the tops are long enough to reach the top of the thigh. Having a scarf handy when visiting historic sites, but especially mosques, is advisable.

If you do wish to wear local clothes it is very welcome and you will find thousands of shops in Lahore which have both 'ready-made'/pret clothes and 'unstitched' fabric. Ready-made can be bought off the rack and unstitched is fabric which can be taken to a tailor. There are a large number of design houses in Pakistan with shops in Lahore which have new designs each season (winter (cambric) and summer (lawn)). The two main types of clothing are *shalwar kameez*, worn by both men and women which is a long, loose-fitting top over cotton trousers, or a *kurta* which is a shorter top which can be worn with jeans, or any other trouser. Most people who wear Pakistani clothes love them instantly. Stylish and beautiful but without the tight, form hugging, judgemental waistbands of western wear.

One last note...no matter what you pack it is likely you will be underdressed in Lahore. Pakistan is one of the few countries which still does glamour on a daily basis. Women wear high heels, makeup, and lots of jewellery. Men wear tailor made suits, silk pocket scarves, and have their leather shoes hand stitched.

The point here is that there is absolutely no need to rush out and buy Indiana Jones-eque travel gear. Lahore is a major metropolitan city not the jungles of Borneo and you will never have need to unzip your trousers into shorts.

Arriving & Getting Around

All nationalities need a visa to enter Pakistan. There is no 'visa on arrival'. Visit/tourist visas may only be arranged in your country of origin or in a country in which you have resident status. This means that if you are a French person living in Nairobi you cannot go to the Pakistan embassy in Nairobi and get a visa. They will require you to get it in Paris. Additionally, if you live in a country like the U.S. where there are several Pakistani consulates, you will have to apply at the correct consulate which covers your area of residence. If you are a resident of Illinois, for example, you will have to apply at the consulate in Chicago and cannot apply in Washington, DC. Visa fees are anywhere between $20 and $200 USD depending on nationality. Having Israeli or Indian stamps in your passport is viewed unfavourably. Indian nationals and military personnel will normally be required to complete additional forms. Visa processing can be done very quickly or take months so it's best to plan ahead.

By Air: Allama Iqbal International Airport is named after Pakistan's national poet. It is located at the eastern edge of Lahore and conveniently placed for most of the city, with a drive to the centre taking around 20 minutes if traffic is light. It is the second largest airport in Pakistan and has three terminals with 25 airlines connecting to 44 cities worldwide. It is best to have arranged a pick up from the airport in advance as many international flights arrive in the middle of the night and taxis and drivers will charge an exorbitant rate. Most hotels can arrange an airport pick up for you. Flight times change in the winter months as Lahore is subject to a thick fog at night and in the morning hours, which means that planes can neither land nor take off. There are no entry nor exit taxes.

Private Car Hire: The easiest way to get around Lahore is with your own car and driver. Even if you enjoy driving you might want to employ a driver for your time in Lahore. Traffic in Lahore is chaotic, aggressive and appears to follow no rules whatsoever. And, while traffic can be terrible in Lahore sometimes for no reason at all, it is especially bad during morning/evening rush hours and dinner time (8pm-12am) on weekends. In addition, there are rarely enough parking spaces wherever you are intending to go so being able to be dropped and picked up will save you valuable time.

If you are visiting for a few days a car and driver can easily be arranged through your hotel. You will need to ensure that the driver speaks English as many do not. Renting a 'saloon' car (e.g. Toyota Corolla) will cost approximately $50 USD per day with a driver.

Uber: the global taxi company, has recently launched in Pakistan with their first city being Lahore. Uber works the same as in other countries where users sign up for the app and input a credit card that is charged after each use. Pre-screened drivers then pick up passengers and are paid by Uber. In Lahore, it's also possible to pay in cash.

Careem: If you'd prefer to use a Pakistani company, then Careem (www.careem.com/lahore/node) works much like Uber. Drivers are pre-screened and picked using an app.

If you don't have a car or use Uber, then your means of getting around will either be taxi, rickshaw (tuk tuk, Qui Qui), or metro bus.

Taxis: There aren't many taxi companies in Lahore but two you should know: Daewoo cabs (daewoocab.com.pk) can be called or booked online and Metro Cab (metrocab.com.pk)

Rickshaws (TukTuks): There are a number of different kinds of rickshaws in Lahore. The first is the *Qui Qui* (pronounced: ching-chi) which has two rows of passenger seats. The second are the CNG rickshaws that run on gas. The new ones have green bodies while the older ones are blue. The old, blue body ones are being phased out and are no longer allowed in some of the higher-end neighbourhoods like the Cantt, DHA and Gulberg. Qui Qui's are also not allowed in these areas. Best to hire a green rickshaw if you want to get all around town.

Metrobus: A convenient way to get around Lahore and well used. The Metrobus is 27 km of track, some of which is elevated, to get buses around traffic. Buses follow known routes and there are 27 stops. Tickets must be purchased prior to riding metro bus and this can be done at each station where there is either a ticket office or ticket machine. For multiple journeys, cards can be purchased and topped up. Metrobus runs from 6.15am to 10.00pm. The closest metrobus stop is Muslim Town stop and the cost is 20 PKR. An interactive map with all the stops can be viewed online (whitengreen.com/blog-98-metro-bus-service-lahore-route-map-and-stop-stations).

Culture & Religion

Pakistan is an Islamic country with most of the population being Muslim. Sunni Muslims are the majority with Shias being a minority. There are also substantial minorities of Hindus, Sikhs, and Christians. While Pakistan has a socially conservative culture it is not necessarily always religiously conservative, and different individuals choose to practice their religion in different ways. You will meet very devout Muslims who are not religiously conservative and devout Muslims who are. You will meet Muslims who are not practicing the religion at all. The issues of religion and culture are extremely dynamic in Pakistan. While there are issues of poverty, violence, education, women's rights, and minority rights this has not stopped women from having a prominent role in society. Women drive, go to school, run businesses, are involved in politics and are active in all arenas of life. Some of them cover their heads and some do not. The best thing to do is not to put Pakistan in a box. Visit, be respectful, and enjoy getting to know the culture. Below are a few cultural tips:

- Alcohol not readily available except in a few hotel bars and private homes. Speaking about drinking or drunkenness is frowned on.
- Few women smoke and those that do rarely do so in public.
- Pork products are not available.
- The call to prayer occurs five times a day and during it other loud music or celebration will often cease.
- Women do not always shake hands with men. If you are a woman greeting a man let him extend his hand first.
- You will often be offered tea or drinks. It is considered polite to accept and engage in polite small talk before proceeding to business.
- When visiting someone's home bring a small gift—flowers, a box of chocolates, a cake from a bakery, or a small houseware item (vase, picture frame, etc.) are all acceptable. Alcohol should not be brought as a gift unless you are sure the hosts drink it, and even then it should be given in private so as not to offend other guests.

Islam in Pakistan

Islam in Pakistan has both religious and political components. When it arrived in the early 700s, it was linked to ruling empires and kingdoms the most famous of which was the Mughal Empire based in Lahore.

Today, Islam is the state religion of Pakistan: the state was founded to protect the rights of a then-Muslim minority in a Hindu-dominated India.

Within Islam there are different sects. Approximately 80% of the Muslims in Pakistan are followers of the Sunni sect and 20% are Shia. Within these two broad sects are different schools of belief. For example, amongst the Sunnis there are Hanafi, Braelvi and Deobandi schools of thought. There are smaller sects such as the Ismailis and the smaller Ahmadi minority which do not easily fit within the two largest sects (the latter were declared non-Muslims in Pakistan in 1974). There is also Sufism—a mystical school which is predominantly Sunni but practiced by some Shia.

FESTIVALS, HOLIDAYS & EVENTS

Important dates in Lahore

Throughout the year, Lahore hosts a number of social and cultural events and celebrates a number of important holidays. It is important to know about these even if you don't plan on attending as it can affect traffic, and what shops or offices might be open.

Pakistan follow two calendars—the lunar, Islamic (Hijri) calendar for religious holidays or events and the solar, Western (Gregorian) calendar for day-to-day activity and government events. This makes many of the religious holidays 'moveable feasts' as they will fall approximately 10 days earlier each year against the Western calendar. Many religious holidays are based on a moon sighting so it is not possible to tell in advance on what day the holiday will fall. Religious dates are placed against an approximate, Western calendar month below (for 2016/7) and marked with a * below. You many check online for an estimate of when the date will fall before travelling.

It is not appropriate for foreigners to participate in, or observe, all of these events and there can be security concerns around them so make sure to check with your hotel or someone local before you do so.

Protests & Demonstrations

Public protest is common in Lahore. Nearly every day, one or more public demonstrations is held by students, trade unions, civil society groups, or people upset about everything from low wages to lack of electricity. The usual sites of these protests are at the Press Club (Usmania colony), near a government building on Mall Road (usually near Faisal Chowk), or another media or government building. Protests and demonstrations are normally no cause for concern. They rarely become large or violent, and while they can block roads and cause inconvenience they are usually easily avoided.

JANUARY

01 January: New Year (public holiday) Most shops and government offices will be closed.

FEBRUARY

JUMADA AL-AWWAL

05 February: Kashmir Day (public holiday) Most shops and government offices will be closed. Demonstrations are held over the continuing disputed territory of Kashmir.

End of February/March: Basant [see box on next pages] Basant is a Punjabi festival marking the coming of spring. While kite-flying is banned there are still decorations up around the city as well as floats and decorations on the canal. Yellow is the colour of Basant and used to be commonly worn during the festival.

February: Lahore Literary Festival (lahorelitfest.com)—an annual event usually in the third week of February, bringing together writers and readers, artists, poets and politicians. This is a lively three days of discussion, book signing and other literary and artistic events.

JUMADA AL-AKHIRAH

MARCH

Spring: Lahore Fashion Week: Created and run by the Pakistan Fashion Design Council (pfdc.org). This is an annual event showcasing the latest fashion from Pakistani designers.

Early March: The National Horse and Cattle Show—held in Fortress Stadium. A week of activities including a livestock display, horse and camel dances, tent pegging, and folk dances from all regions of Pakistan.

23 March: Pakistan Day (public holiday) Ceremonies held at Iqbal's tomb and Minar-e-Pakistan.

APRIL

RAJAB

Spring: Lahore Music Meet (lahoremusicmeet.com) is a two-day event dedicated to the celebration and critique of music in Pakistan. LMM aims to bring together enthusiasts, artisans, artists, patrons, industry representatives and academics to initiate dialogue on the developments in music.

SHABAN

MAY

*April/May: The Festival of Lights (Mela Chiraghan) is held each year to mark the death anniversary (urs) of the famous Punjabi Sufi writer, Shah Hussain. The three-day event is held at the saint's shrine about five minutes west of Shalimar Gardens. Devotees sing, dervishes dance and there are poetry recitals at times. The festival centres around a large bonfire into which people place oil and candles. Women rarely attend the first two days, as the third day is open especially for them.

01 May: Labour Day (public holiday)

*Ramazan (Urdu pronunciation of Ramadhan) begins: A month of fasting from the morning prayer to sundown each day. Restaurants will be closed during the day, and open between dusk and dawn. Shops will open late and close at various times. It is best not to eat or drink in public during the day while people are fasting. The iftar meal, which ends the fast, begins right after sunset prayers. This is a big social occasion, and many Lahoris love to go out to eat making restaurants very busy. Make reservations!

JUNE

RAMADAN

*Eid-ul-Fitr (public holiday): This is a 2-3 day festival ends Ramazan. This is a major event and a lot of shops/restaurants open and close at different times than normal. People will take holiday time to travel and be with their family.

SHAWWAL

JULY

AUGUST

DHUL QADAH

14 August: Independence Day (public holiday) celebrating Independence from the British and the creation of the modern-day Pakistani state.

DHUL HIJJAH

SEPTEMBER

*Eid al Azha (public holiday) A celebration of Abraham's offer to sacrifice his son Ishmael. It is customary to sacrifice an animal such as a sheep or a cow, and share the meat with family, friends and the poor.

September: Naqsh School of Arts (facebook.com/NaqshSchoolofArts) has a yearly exhibition of their graduating class.

OCTOBER

MUHARRAM

*Muharram begins with Ashura - a month (40 days) of mourning for Shia Muslims related to death of the Prophet's grandson Hussein during the battle of Karbala in 680 AD. It is a sombre affair with large processions of people who whip themselves and mourn in public. The routes of these parades are published in advance and should be avoided as they have been targeted for sectarian violence in the past.

SAFAR

NOVEMBER

*Chehlum - the final day of Muharram which will include processions, and prayers at Shia mosques.

November: The World Performing Arts Festival is held at the Al Hamra cultural complex and is a ten-day festival consisting of musicals, theatre, concerts, dance, solo, mime and puppetry shows.

09 November: Muhammad Iqbal's birthday—semi-official so some business/government will be closed. A celebration of Pakistan's most famous poet and philosopher who is considered very instrumental in the Pakistan movement.

Daachi Foundation Arts & Crafts Exhibition: Each year the Daachi Foundation has an Arts and Crafts Exhibition which brings together different artisans, businesses and NGOs selling their handicrafts. It normally runs for two weeks and is held at Tollinton Museum.

DECEMBER

RABI AL-AWWAL

*Eid Milad Un-Nabi (public holiday) a celebration of the birth of the Prophet (PBUH) where lots of public buildings will be draped in lights.

25 December: Christmas Day and the birthday of Quaid-e-Azam (Jinnah) (public holiday)

RABI AL-AKHAR

Basant

"I cannot recall anything that thrilled me more than kite flying in my boyhood days. Whenever I observed my kite soaring towards the clouds, I experienced a sense of power and mastery over the elements. Perhaps, in a way, I identified myself with the kite itself flying so free and so high above me, far from the madding crowd, enveloping me in a spirit of freedom and adventure. I felt that kites also signified a hope, a desire for escape, fancy dreams entrusted to a breath of wind and connected to a string and the hand that clasped it."   – Pran Nevile

Basant—the Punjabi festival celebrating spring—used to be known for immense kite-flying competitions which took place on the rooftops and in parks throughout the city. During the week of the festival, the entire city would celebrate by taking to the streets and rooftops to watch kite-flying competitions, and Lahore's skies were crowded with kites. The Old City was at the heart of the celebrations, as parties with music, food, and dance went on all night while hundreds of thousands of kites were flown.

In addition to kite-flying, kite-fighting was also common. Rivals used kite string (*dori*) coated with glue and ground glass, manoeuvering their kites to cross and cut the string of their opponents. When a kite string was cut people would yell, '*bo-kata*' and children would race through the streets to be the first to collect the downed kite as it wafted toward the ground. Each neighbourhood (*mohalla*) in the Old City would have its expert—usually a teenaged boy, known as a *khilari*—who would reign in kite fighting. An entire industry existed around kite flying and Basant, with thousands from the diaspora returning to Lahore for the celebrations.

Each year, however, the festivities resulted in death and injury as children fell from roofs, kite strings fell across roads and injured motorcyclists, brought down electricity wires and celebratory gunfire wreaked havoc. Citing these reasons, the Lahore government banned kite-flying in 2007. However, you will be pressed to find a Lahori who doesn't mourn its departure.

WHERE TO STAY

Book your Lahore base

While there are plenty of places to stay in Lahore the city is not known for its hotel and guest house selection and only a few are mentioned here. That said, more are popping up all the time, and even AirBnB has started listings for Lahore but these should be checked for authenticity before booking. It is possible to find a place to stay anywhere in the range of $20-$30 USD per night all the way up to $1,000 USD. As with most things, you get what you pay for. With the exception of a few outliers, hotels in Lahore are considered mid-range both in terms of price and amenities offered.

Because there are so many hotels in Lahore and there is no independent assessment, we are relying on TripAdvisor ratings and our own visits to recommend where to stay.

Many organisations that bring visitors to Pakistan–either on tours, or for business—have strict security requirements and only allow their staff to stay at certain hotels. Hotels which we know have been security approved by an international organisation are listed with an * in the list below. This does not mean that they are secure premises and each visitor must take responsibility for their own security.

Pearl Continental

Pearl Continental*
(Price Range - $199-$950 USD per night)
Trip Advisor – #4 of 38 hotels–454 reviews –overall rating 'very good'

The 'PC', as it is known, is located on Mall Road and is considered one of the most secure hotels in Lahore. It is an enormous hotel and has greater security measures than some others. It boasts six restaurants and two cafes along with a 9-hole golf course, pool, heath club, and other amenities.

Website   pchotels.com/PCHL/
Address   Shahrah-e-Quaid-e-Azam (Mall
          Road)
Phone   +92 (0) 42 3636-0210
Email   vpchl@pchotels.com

Avari Hotel*
(Price Range - $170-$500 USD per night)
Trip Advisor - #6 of 38 hotels – 211 reviews –overall rating 'very good'

The Avari is older than the PC and has its own charm. It is also on Mall Road and has five restaurants—Kims, Dynasty, Fujiyama, Tollington, and a café, Cinammon. Different amenities are available with different classes of room but, in general, breakfast, WIFI, use of the gym and pool, and airport shuttle are among those offered.

Website   avari.com
Address   87 Shahrah-e-Quaid-e-Azam
          (Mall Road)
Phone   +92 42 3603 3528
Email   resvlhe@avari.com

The Avari Hotel

Faletti's Hotel Lahore

Faletti's Hotel Lahore*
(Price Range - $110-$430 USD per night)

Just off Mall road behind the Avari and the WAPDA building you'll find this historic hotel which has been operating at the same location since 1880. Breakfast is included as is water, newspaper, WIFI, and an airport pickup arranged in advance. There is a Lebanese restaurant, L'Auberge in the hotel and Café De Brando serving Pakistani and continental food.

Website falettishotel.com
Address 24 Egerton Road
Phone +92 (0) 42 363 63946 / 51
Email info@falettishotel.com

The Residency Hotel*
(Price Range - $125-$200 USD per night)
Trip Advisor - #2 of 38 hotels–110 reviews –overall rating between 'very good' and 'excellent'

Located in a quiet neighbourhood this hotel is off the main drag but still close to Gulberg shopping and eateries . It provides breakfast, bottled water, WIFI, and airport transfers with bookings. They also have a popular gym, swimming pool, and badminton court and '39 Restaurant'.

Website rh.com.pk
Address 39-A, off Zafar Ali Road, Gulberg V
Phone +92 (0) 42 111 395 395
Email booking@rh.com.pk

The Residency Hotel

Website   www.hospitalityinnlahore.com
Address   25 Egerton Road
Phone   +92 42 3631 0077
Email   info@hospitalityinnlahore.com

The Moor Heritage Suites*
(Price Range - $220 - $480 per night)
Trip Advisor - #3 of 38 hotels–22 reviews –overall rating between 'very good' and 'excellent'

The Moor Heritage Suites is a gorgeous property located in Gulberg, very near to Liberty Mall/Market. They have studio, 1-bedroom, and 2-bedroom apartments which make it convenient if traveling with family. Security is good, WIFI and breakfast provided, and there is a gym and small, serene park available to guests.

Website   heritageluxurysuites.com
Address   100-C2, Gulberg 3
Phone   +92 (0) 42 357 15985
Email   reservations@heritageluxurysuites.com

The Nishat Hotel

The Nishat Hotel
(Price Range - $130-$430 USD per night)
Trip Advisor - #5 of 38 hotels in Lahore–51 reviews–overall rating 'very good'

A relative newcomer to Lahore's hotel scene, The Nishat opened in 2014 and calls itself the first boutique hotel in the city. Located in the heart of Gulberg, a stay at Nishat will put you in the centre of the restaurant and shopping action. They have complimentary buffet breakfast, WIFI, and indoor heated pool and gym. There is also The Cube Restaurant, The Pizzeria, and the Cigar Lounge.

Website   nishathotel.com
Address   9A Mian Mahmood Ali Kasuri Rd
          Gulberg III
Phone   +92 42 111-000-777
Email   reservations@nishathotel.com

Hospitality Inn*
Trip Advisor – #1 of 38 hotels–174 reviews –overall rating 'very good'

Close to Faletti's on Egerton Road and not far from Mall Road this is a more budget option but the rooms are clean and well appointed and the staff friendly.

The Moor Heritage Suites

Hotel One*
Trip Advisor - #19 of 38 hotels in Lahore–36 reviews–overall rating 'average'

Run by the Pearl Continental, Hotel One has three hotels in Lahore

Mall Road
Website   hotelone.com.pk/city_12.php
Address   105 - A, Upper Mall
Phone   +92 42 36361001
Email   hotelone.mall@hotelone.com.pk

Gulberg (City)
Website   hotelone.com.pk/city_1.php
Address   40/A-2 Mehmood Ali Kasuri
          Road, Gulberg 3
Phone   +92 42 35773181 – 5
Email   hotelone.hc@hotelone.com.pk

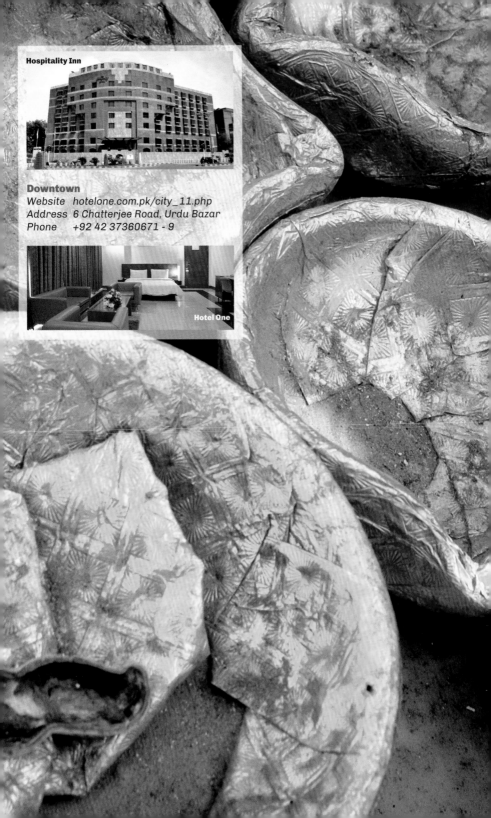

Hospitality Inn

Downtown

Website   hotelone.com.pk/city_11.php
Address 6 Chatterjee Road, Urdu Bazar
Phone   +92 42 37360671 - 9

Hotel One

WHAT TO SEE

Explore Lahore's rich history & culture

The Old City

'Walled City' or 'Inner City' or Anderoon Shehr

Located in the northwest of modern Lahore, the Walled City, or Old City, is the original city of Lahore. Until the British period, there was little outside of the walls of the Old City except the Punjabi plains speckled with tombs and gardens of former Mughals. The area between the Old City and Shalimar gardens was nothing but shrubs and trees and travelling would take around an hour to reach by horseback or nearly two on foot.

It was Emperor Akbar who first built a wall around the city between 1584-1598. The Old City covered about 650 acres (just over 2.5 square kilometres, or one square mile). The walls were 30 feet high but were later brought down to 15 feet before being demolished altogether by the British shortly after they annexed Punjab in 1849. There are differing accounts about why the British felt they needed to destroy the walls. It is likely that they did not want to be shut out of the city in an insurgency but they were also obsessed with fresh air and need bricks for the construction of their own building. (This followed a time honoured tradition in Lahore where successive rulers would tear down, or strip, the buildings of their predecessors to build their own – see 'Conservation' page 63). When the walls were pulled down, the moat, built by Ranjit Singh, was filled in and a ring of parks established around three quarters of the Old City area. Today, the closest you can come to seeing what the walls might have looked like are the walls of the Lahore Fort, which sits in a corner of the Old City.

The streets in the old city are picturesque but dense, dark, and crowded. Old houses (havelis) and new commercial buildings rise up on either sides of streets and alleys—some of which are only wide enough for one person to walk through. While exploring one has to be alert to avoid stepping in an open drain, or being hit by a motorcycle, ox cart or other pedestrians. The streets wind and it's easy to become lost among the hodge podge of different markets and thoroughfares. That said, it's not a particularly big area. It is possible to walk across from one end to the other in less than 20 minutes.

Given the narrow, crowded streets, life in the old city used to concentrate on the rooftops. There, inhabitants could get some fresh air, gossip with neighbours and children could play. Women could be outside without leaving their homes. Street vendors would pass crying out their goods, and families lower baskets to street level to exchange money and products. Before the 1950's there were hardly any homes that were above three or four stories. Now, the houses tower up eight or nine stories high.

Today, approximately 200,000 people live in the 2.5 square kms of the Old City, making it far more densely populated than the rest of Lahore. A person may be born in and live their entire lives in the Old City but they are usually poor. Families who can afford to move to suburban neighbhourhoods in other parts of Lahore. Their vacant homes are either sold or occupied by squatters—usually poor Pashtun migrants from the north of Pakistan who worked in the cloth or shoe trade. Anna Suvorva describes the Old City saying, *"The inhabitants of the Walled City of Lahore too, are not rich: unskilled and semiskilled labourers, petty vendors, craftsmen, and some members of the artistic intelligentsia that use the old buildings as*

ateliers. *The narrow medieval streets in this part of town house no banks, luxury hotels, offices, or other places where money circulates. The traditional bazaar is the Walled City's main economic entity, determining the work patterns of the local inhabitants. The Walled City's state of sanitation is also quite medieval: frequent power outages, a poor sewage system, and a water supply that is unfi for consumption. In spite of its around-the-clock din and commotion, the Aderoon Shehr is slowly but surely dying."*

Havelis of the Old City

Havelis are large houses, or mansions, standing between two and five stories high and mostly found in the Old City. Havelis in the Old City are built close together sharing walls with surrounding buildings. They have flat roofs on which kites used to be flown or where people sleep outside during the hot months. Many also have ornate wooden balconies which overlook the street allowing women in purdah (seclusion) to be in the fresh air without being seen. Each haveli was usually associated with, or built by, a merchant, rich tradesperson, or noble.

There are many examples of havelis which can be visited in the Old City and these are in various states of repair. The restaurants on Heera Mandi's Food Street, like Haveli and Cocoo's Den, are housed in old havelis. The Fakir Khana Museum is also located in an excellent example of an old Haveli. Nau Nihal Singh, the son of Ranjit Singh, built one of the most beautiful and well-known havelis between the Bhatti and Lahori gates. It is a fine example from the Sikh period but has been occupied by the Victoria Girls High School since the 1920s.

Darwaza (Gates) of the Old City

There were 13 ancient gates into the Old City. Six of these still exist today and a *
indicates them in the list below. It is still possible to pass through the thoroughfares
where the 13 gates once stood even if the gate is no longer there. All the gates still
standing date back only to the British period as the Mughal gates were either already
destroyed or were torn down. The sole exception to this is the Roshnai gate built in the
Sikh period.

Masti Gate
'Masti' is likely a distortion of Masjidi or Masit (mosque in Punjabi) and named for the nearby
Maryam Zamani Mosque. The original gate, built by Mughal Emperor Akbar in 1566, opened
onto the river Ravi.

Kashmiri Gate *
This gate opens northward in the direction of Kashmir
and also once opened onto the Ravi. Some of the busiest
commercial areas of the Old City are located immediately
inside this gate.

Sheranwala Gate *
Legend says that Ranjit Singh used to keep lions near this
gate and lions used to be seen in the plasterwork. A ferry
service on the River Ravi used to stop at this gate. The gate
was also called the Khizri gate, after the patron saint of
waters.

Yakki Gate
The name Yakki is likely a reference to 'Zaki', a saint and
martyr who died fighting the Mongols. Legend says that even
after decapitation in battle his body continued to fight on.

Delhi Gate *
This is one of the main gates used to access the Old City today. Named as it faces Delhi, there
is a corresponding Lahori Gate in old Delhi. The path through the Delhi gate was wide and
important, given that trade with Delhi came to the city through it. The Walled City Authority
has a small office in the gate and most tourists enter the Old City here. Immediately inside
the gate are areas where conservation of the Old City has been concentrated. It is also the
approach to the Wazir Khan Mosque and the Shahi Hamams.

Akbari Gate
Don't confuse this gate with the Akbar
gate which sits on the eastern side of the
Lahore Fort. This Akbari gate was named
after the first Mughal Emperor, Akbar,
who ruled from 1556. It is thought to
have been one of the earliest structures
the Mughals built in Lahore.

Mochi Gate
This gate was likely a mispronunciation
of the word 'Moti', meaning pearl. It
was named after an officer in Emperor
Akbar's court.

Shah Alami Gate

Named for Emperor Aurangzeb's son who ruled for a few years following Aurangzeb's death in the early 1700's. The gate was destroyed in the Partition riots.

Lahori Gate *

Facing southward toward the rest of Lahore city this is another main gate. As the Mughal Empire decline all but three gates in the Old City were bricked in. This gate was one which remained open. When Ranjit Singh conquered Lahore he entered the city through this gate. When the British rebuilt the gates in 1864 this was the only gate that closely resembled its original design.

Mori Gate

A small gate that used for ridding the city of rubbish and refuse.

Bhati Gate *

Named for the Bhatti tribe who lived near the gate. Touring circuses and theatre companies congregated around, and just outside of, the gate

Taxili Gate

The Royal Mint, or Taxal, was located near the gate during the Mughal period.

Roshnai Gate *

The 'Gate of Light' is the oldest gate in the Fort wall built by Emperor Akbar. The gate was always kept illuminated at night.

Lahore sprawls; its epicentre keeps changing. It is hard to imagine that the town both in itself and as capital of several vagrant empires was once contained within its walls and bustling gates: the Old City, as it is known, has luckily escaped a museum or a mausoleum atmosphere, and remains instead a node of obsessive activity or pleasure. Whether its getting or spending involves wreathes and garlands, jewellery and garments, dancing and singing, piety and prostitution, but it still approximates what may be best named as a frenetic trading in joy. When the Old City withers, they say, so will Lahore. And thus its gates—such as the Alumgiri Gate, the Batti Gate— continue to contain, invisibly, that curious phenomenon, which is the integrity of Lahore.

—Sara Suleri Goodyear, *Lahore Remembered*

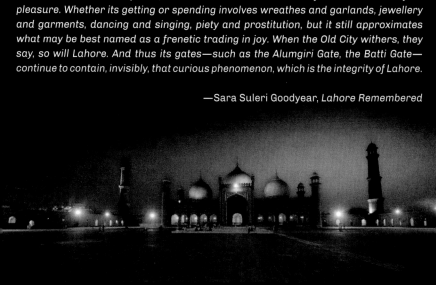

Lahore Fort (Shahi Qila) - UNESCO World Heritage Site

Located in the northwest corner of the Old City the Lahore Fort is one of the primary attractions for visitors in Lahore. No one knows how long a fort has been on the site but the present structure was started during the reign of Mughal Emperor Akbar between 1556-1605. Subsequent features were added later by Emperors Jahangir and Shah Jahan. It is one of the few buildings that contains all the different phases of Mughal architecture. Both Sikh and British rulers would continue to use the fort while ruling Lahore as it was a prime way to keep an eye on the comings and goings of the city. The fort is approximately 50 enclosed acres and contains a number of interesting structures, including the exquisite Sheesh Mahal (Palace of Mirrors), intricately inlaid with coloured stone, glass, and mirrors. Make sure to take note of the tile mosaics at the entrance. The large, white Alamgiri gate built in 1674 used to be the main access between Badshahi Mosque, Hazuri Bagh and the Fort. It is best viewed from the Hazuri Bagh. This gate is now closed and visitors need to access each site by an independent gate and footpath.

Visiting: Lahore Fort is open daily for tourists from approximately 8am to 6pm (daylight hours). There is a small entrance fee of 20 rupees for Pakistanis and 500 rupees for foreigners, which is paid at a ticket booth.

Badshahi Masjid (Mosque)—tentative UNESCO World Heritage Site

A few hundred metres to the west of Lahore Fort is the Badshahi Mosque. It is the second largest mosque in Pakistan (after Faisal Mosque in Islamabad) and the fifth largest in the world. It is also known as Alamgiri Masjid. The courtyard is 85,000 square meters and said to accommodate over a hundred thousand people. It was built in 1671 by the sixth Mughal Emperor Aurangzeb, nearly a century after the Lahore Fort. Constructed in red sandstone it is often compared to the Jama Masjid in Delhi. Its beauty, elegance, symmetry and technical perfection epitomise the cultural achievements of the Mughal era. The rooms found in the corridors surrounding the mosque courtyard used to be part of the madrassa (seminary). Your guide should point out the incredible acoustics of the main prayer hall. Rooftop restaurants like Cooco's Den, Haveli, and Andaaz provide an incomparable view of the mosque, especially at dusk.

There is a museum of sorts in the outer wall of the mosque near the gate, which houses some of the oldest Islamic relics in South Asia. Deemed Fakir gifts, a turban, coat, sandals, and quilt of the Prophet (PBUH), as well as Caliph Ali's (the Prophet's son-in-law) turban, amulet and Fatimah's (the Prophet's daughter) veil and prayer rug are held here.

Visiting: The mosque is open daily for worshippers and visitors usually between about 8am and 6pm (daylight hours). Women should bring a scarf to cover their heads while inside. There is no entrance fee, although visitors need to leave their shoes at the entrance and a small tip will be expected when retrieving them. Visitors should also be respectful about speaking and taking photographs during prayer times.

"But it also remains a moment of glad necessity, for who can conjure up a vision of Lahore without remembering the tiny droplet of beauty that is Iqbal's tomb, resting in the shade of Badshahi Mosque? He deserves that spot. Lahore is a city of untold monuments: in other words, a space startling with the stories it can tell. The Badshahi remains for me the most perfect of mosques, so that each time I visit it I am frozen again by the ninety-nine names of God, as though I were reading them for the first time."

- Sara Suleri Goodyear
Lahore Remembered

Hazuri Bagh & Baradari (Garden & Pavilion)

Between the Lahore Fort and Badshahi Mosque is a garden that was a waiting area for both. The white, marble pavilion which stands in the middle was built by Ranjit Singh. Originally, it was two-storey but a lightning strike in 1932 collapsed the upper story. Recent investigations indicate there were also subterranean chambers where the court could enjoy cooler temperatures.

Visiting: The area outside Badshahi Mosque which contains this garden is usually open between 8am and 6pm (daylight hours). There is no entrance fee.

Tomb of Allama Muhammad Iqbal

In the Hazuri Bagh, to the left of the entrance to Badshahi Mosque is the tomb of Allama Muhammad Iqbal. Iqbal was an Urdu poet and philosopher credited for inspiring the creation of Pakistan. He died in 1938 and the tomb completed in 1940. The small, sandstone pavilion is a combination of Afghan and Moorish styles. Each year, on Iqbal's birthday (November 9) a different branch of the Pakistan military takes over the guarding of the tomb.

Visiting: The area outside Badshahi Mosque which contains this garden is usually open between 8am and 6pm (daylight hours). At times, the tomb will be shut and visitors are not allowed. There is no entrance fee.

Shahi Hamam (Baths)

Close to Delhi gate, you will find the Shahi Hamam. Recently renovated by the Aga Khan Foundation, the hamam is a Turkish-style, public bath built in 1634 by Wazir Khan who also built the Wazir Khan mosque. This is the only surviving hamam on the south Asian subcontinent and includes restored frescoes and exposed hot and cold pools and steam rooms.

Visiting: The hamam is open daily for tourists from 9am to sunset (daylight hours). There is an entrance fee of 500 rupees per person for foreigners.

Maryam Zamani's Masjid (Mosque)

The oldest mosque in Lahore, built between 1611 and 1615, is tucked away in a neighbourhood opposite the Akbari gate of the Old City. There are conflicting accounts of Maryam Zamani's identity. She was either a wife of Emperor Akbar, or mother or wife of Emperor Jahangir. Jahangir's mother was named Jodhabai but it is unclear if she and Maryam Zamani were the same person. The access to the mosque is just barely visible from Fort Road. Navigate through some tire and mechanic shops to find it. Ranjit Singh did turn it into a gunpowder factory and after its restoration little preservation was done. Despite this the original tilework is still visible.

Visiting: The mosque is usually open during daylight hours but locked at night. There is no entrance fee although visitors need to leave their shoes at the entrance and there is no one to mind them. If this concerns, put them in a bag and carry them with you. Visitors should be respectful about speaking and photography.

Sunehri Masjid (Golden Mosque)

Built in 1753 by Mughalani Begum, the widow of the Governor of Lahore this mosque is commonly called the Golden Mosque as it is recognised by three gold-plated domes. Mughalani was an interesting figure who heavily involved herself in political intrigue. The deputy governor was one of her favourites until, according to Anna Suvorova, their story ended unhappily. He fell from favour and the widow ordered her servants to beat him to death with their slippers. The mosque itself incorporates Sikh architecture and stands in the midst of a busy market in the Old City, making it difficult to observe except from the inside.

Visiting: The mosque is supposed to be open daily for visitors during daylight hours but often it is locked. There is no entrance fee although visitors need to leave their shoes at the entrance and there is no one to mind them. If this concerns, put them in a bag and carry them with you. Visitors should be respectful about speaking and photography of those praying.

Wazir Khan Masjid (Mosque)—tentative UNESCO World Heritage Site

This mosque is a gem which should not be missed. Located in the Old City, not far from Delhi Gate, the mosque was built in 1634-1635 by Wazir Khan, nobleman in the court of Mughal Emperor Shah Jahan. Wazir Khan would eventually become the Governor of Lahore and the mosque was built in an under-developed area of the city, which allowed a large chowk (market area) to be established in front of it. The area became a social, commercial and political hub for hundreds of years. Wazir Khan built a house in the area and other nobles seemed encouraged to do the same.

The proposed site of the Wazir Khan Mosque already housed the tomb of Miran Badshah and the tomb of another Sufi saint, Syad Suf. Both of these tombs were preserved in the construction of the mosque and can still be visited.

The mosque is known for its beautiful, coloured tilework and calligraphy, both considered some of the finest remaining from the Mughal period. Rudyard Kipling's father, the first principal of the National College of Arts, was so taken with the mosque that he required his students spent time there sketching and modeling it. The minarets, if accessible, provide a bird's eye view of the Old City.

Visiting: The mosque is open daily for tourists from 8am to 6pm (daylight hours). Restoration work is currently being undertaken. There is no entrance fee, although visitors need to leave their shoes at the entrance and a small tip will be expected when retrieving them. Visitors should also be respectful about speaking and photography during prayer times.

Malik Ayaz's Tomb

Malik Ayaz was a slave during the Ghaznavid Empire who rose to prominence to be the Governor of Lahore. He is famously believed to have been the lover of Sultan Mahmud Ghaznavi. Lahore became a prominent cultural centre during his reign, and he is credited with being the first ruler to build a wall completely around the Old City.

Ayaz is famously referenced by Pakistan's national poet, Allama Iqbal, as an example of the equality of all men in Islam. Roughly translated it says: "*Mahmood the king and slave Ayaz, in line, as equals, stood arrayed. The lord was no more lord to slave: while both to the One Master prayed.*"

Visiting: Malik Ayaz's Tomb is in the Old City near the Rang Mahal area. The gates are frequently locked. Entrance is free.

Rang Mahal Mission School

Rang Mahal Christian School is the oldest school in Lahore. The school was founded in 1949 in a building called Rang Mahal which was built in the early to mid-1600's. It sits in the midst of one of the old city's busiest markets.

Visiting: As a functioning school it is necessary to request permission to visit from the administration. Visit their website for more details and contact information: peb.edu.pk/RangMahal

Mongols, Mughals, and Muggles

For those of us who were never taught Central Asian history, and for those of us who have forgotten our Central Asian history, and for those of us who are avid Harry Potter fans a little help distinguishing between Mongol, Mughals, and Muggles is in order. First, let's deal with the easy one: Muggles. Muggles are characters with non-magical parents created by J.K. Rowling in her Harry Potter book series. To the best of our knowledge Muggles have never had anything to do with Lahore.

Likewise, the Mongol link to Lahore is tenuous. The Mongol Empire — infamously ruled by Ghengis Khan and Kublai Khan—existed throughout the 1200's to early 1300's. Only a few Mongol armies made it to Lahore and they had no staying power.

The Mughals, however, followed several hundred years later and were distantly related to the famous Ghengis being descendants on his wife's side. The Mughals had a profound effect on Lahore building some of its most famous sites as well as many in what is now India—including the Taj Mahal.

Iqbal Park & Minar-e-Pakistan

Iqbal Park (formerly Minto Park) is a large park in which there are two important sites. The Minar-e-Pakistan and the Samadhi of Ranjit Singh. The minar (minaret) is a 60-metre tall monument built to commemorate the passing of the Lahore Resolution in March 1940. The three-day general assembly called for greater autonomy for Muslims in India during British rule which is regarded as the first demand for a separate Muslim state. The minar may be viewed from Lahore Fort as well as from the ring road around the Old City.

Visiting: It used to be possible to climb the Minar but it has been closed to visitors for some time.

Samadhi of Ranjit Singh

The Samadhi (place of cremation) of Ranjit Singh is also located in Iqbal park and is a complex of chambers and buildings with pronounced white domes and gold gilding. All these buildings are fine examples of period Sikh architecture with domes more ornate than those favoured by the Mughals. The site also has a shrine to Guru Arjan, the 5th Sikh guru, who was arrested during the reign of Jahangir and due to be beheaded. However, it is believed that when he stepped down to the river to perform his ablutions he disappeared into the earth.

Visiting: Due to religious and security concerns it is only possible to view the Samadhi from outside the locked gates unless you are Sikh, or carry an Indian passport. Some guides are able to get access but best to check in advance.

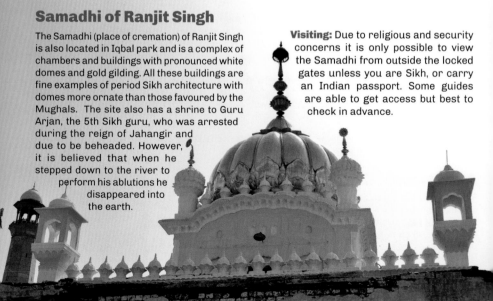

Qutb-ud-Din Aibak's Tomb

One of the oldest tombs in Lahore, this is the final resting place of the first Muslim Emperor of the subcontinent. Born a Turkish slave, Qutb-ud-Din Aibak rose to rule in 1206. He died playing chaugan—a precursor to polo—in 1210. The tomb was reconstructed between 1971 and 1984 so the construction is new.

Visiting: The tomb is easy to find in Anarkali, a few minutes' walk across the ring road from the Lahori Gate of the Old City. It sits in a small garden next to the road. Often the door to the masoleum is locked so let your guide know if you want to see inside.

Conservation Efforts

"The city, however, does not tell its past, but contains it like the lines of a hand, written in the corners of the streets, the gratings of the windows, the banisters of the steps..."

– Italo Calvino

Visitors to Lahore are often surprised by the dilapidated state of historic sites as well as their continued defacement by the public. Unlike in other countries where ancient history is protected behind glass and barriers, it is still possible to climb on, and touch, ancient buildings and relics in Lahore.

While it is a tragedy that these sites are crumbling and fading, it is important to remember that their decline is not a recent development. Successive empires did no favours stripping them of precious metals, stones and bricks so they could build their own. Several sites, including the Tomb of Noor Jahan are said to have been stripped by Ranjit Singh to build the Golden Temple in Amritsar. The British tore down the walls of the Old City as they needed bricks to build their own buildings outside its gates.

The concept of conserving—instead of plundering—sites is a relatively new concept. Perhaps only a hundred years old. Conservation efforts depend on educating people about the benefits of preserving heritage, as well as a government with funds to make that possible. Both of these have been slowly growing in Lahore. Conservation has to compete with other priorities like income, transportation and housing.

Certain advocates, individuals and foundations are working to conserve historic Lahore. The most prominent of these is the Lahore Conservation Society (lcs.org.pk) which is dedicated to the protection, conservation and improvement of Lahore's physical environment. They have talks and trips from time to time so it is worth checking their website. Also, the Walled City Authority has made some effort to restore historic sites in the Old City (walledcitylahore.gop.pk), especially through the introduction of modern water and sewage which helps to preserve infrastructure.

Shah Salman Sirhindi has produced an excellent short video on conservation in the Old City called Future of the Past and the Walled City Authority's documentary on conservation of the old city. Both can be found through a Google search.

You can help conservation efforts by not causing further degradation of the sites. Refrain from walking on, or touching, buildings and facades even if other people are doing so. Support the different projects aimed at raising awareness of heritage sites in Pakistan.

Jahangir's Tomb

The tomb of the fourth Mughal Emporer, Jahangir is located in Shahdara, a small town on the other side of the river Ravi from the Old City. The tomb sits in a garden complex built in about 1627 by his wife, Noor Jahan. The garden's layout follows a pattern of sixteen squares divided by brick walkways, water channels and fountains. Upon entering you are surrounded by the Akbari Serai (traveller's inn) which has 180 small rooms that provided accomodation for travellers as well as offices for officials working there. The complex also contains the tomb of Asif Jah, brother of Noor Jahan and father of Mumtaz Mahal. Mumtaz married Jahangir's son, Shah Jahan, and when she died in childbirth he constructed the Taj Mahal in which to bury her. Asif Jah's tomb was originally covered in marble, but this was reportedly stripped during Ranjit Singh's reign. Noor Jahan, whose name means 'Light of the World', is buried in a mausoleum close by. In order to reach it you must leave the complex and cross a park and road. The Lahore to Rawalpindi rail line runs through the once famous rose garden surrounding her tomb.

Visiting: The complex is open during daylight hours and costs 500 rupees. A ticket booth is located in the main gate. When entering the mausoleum itself visitors will need to remove their shoes and a small tip will be expected for the guard watching them.

As good a place as any to be dead

The living accommodate the dead in some interesting ways in Lahore. For example, when Mohammed Kasim Khan, a cousin of Mughal Emperor Akbar, died in 1635 a grand tomb was built. The Sikhs put barracks in the gardens and when the British arrived they turned it into what it is today, Government house. The tomb remains right inside the house. In gardens and buildings throughout the city you will find tombs of the city's predecessors while the business of living goes on around them.

Kamran's Baradari (Pavilion)

The River Ravi used to flow directly by the Fort but its course was changed by river works. Kamran's Baradari used to sit on the right bank of the river but became isolated on a new island when the river's course shifted. In the 1800's a 'boat bridge' connected the two sides of the river with fishing boats tethered together and a walking bridge constructed over the top. The baradari is thought to have been constructed around 1540 by Kamran Mirza, the son of the first Mughal Emperor Babur. But, some attribute its construction to the period of Shah Jahan. It was built in the style of most baradaris, two-storied with 12 arches. It has been heavily restored/reconstructed.

Visiting: It is only possible to get to the island by boat and there is a car park just before the AH1 New Ravi bridge crossing. A rowboat crossing costs approximately 500 PKR.

Lahore Railway Station

Most visitors to Lahore aren't taking a train so they miss the hectic chaos of this historic station. Built in 1859 by the British it was the headquarter of Pakistan railways. It resembles a fort because it was intended to be one if necessary in an emergency. Trains used to run through the station to India, but only one does so today, the Samjhota Express. Trains do, however, still run both locally and to/from Karachi and Peshawar. Watching the hectic chaos as trains come and go can be a cultural experience in its own right.

Visiting: The railway station is always open although there is a heavier police presence at night. Few foreigners visit the railway station and major infrastructure is still maintained as a state secret to, you might be questioned if taking pictures.

Bibi Pak Daman Shrine

Less well known than either the Data Darbar or Mian Mir shrines is Bibi Pak Daman. Legend says that the mausoleum contains the grave of six pious women related to the Prophet (PBUH) who came to Lahore after the Karbala tragedy from which the Shia/Sunni split began. Legend also maintains that Data Ganj Baksh was a devotee and frequented the shrine. The shrine is tucked away in a cemetery off Empress road across from the Police Lines.

Visiting: The cemetery in which the shrine is located is open during hours of daylight. The shrine becomes busier during the Islamic month of Muharram (when the tragedy of Karbala is commemorated) as well as during the urs (death anniversary) of Bibi Pak which is currently in the spring but moves according to the Islamic calendar.

Mian Mir Shrine

Mian Mir is one of two well known shrines in Lahore. It is quieter than Data Darbar but equally important as it is believed to protect the city. Mian Mir was a Sufi saint who lived in the late 1500's and his tomb was built in the early 1600's. He was the spiritual teacher of Dara Shikoh, Shah Jahan's eldest son. Mian Mir was friends with the 5th Sikh Guru, Arjan, and it is believed that Arjan invited him to lay the foundation stone of the Sri Harmandir Sahib (Golden Temple) in Amritsar. The area around the shrine was named Mian Mir by the British when they built their cantonment there. The shrine itself is small, quiet, and charming; the courtyard filled with birds that often take flight as people move about.

Visiting: The shrine is open during daylight hours and can be busier on Thursdays as well as during the 'urs' (death anniversary) of Mian Mir—19th/20th December. If approaching the shrine you will need to remove your shoes.

Data Darbar Shrine

Data Darbar is perhaps Lahore's most famous, and always-busy Sufi shrine. Located just across the Old City Ring Road near the Bhati gate it contains the tomb of a Sufi saint known locally as Data Ganj Baksh. Baksh lived in the 11th century and is considered Lahore's patron saint. It is one of the oldest shrines in South Asia and people arriving in Lahore often stop here first to pay homage, ask for blessings, and pray. The shrine is known for its calligraphy which was done in 1997 by a newly established guild of master calligraphers who work to preserve the art. The shrine is active day and night, and positively heaving during festivals. During these, Sufi music will be played and dancing held. In 2010, two suicide bombers targeted the site and many people were killed and injured.

Visiting: While the shrine is always open the best time to visit is early in the morning to avoid crowds. There is very little parking available so it is best to be dropped and picked. Take care of your possessions and belongings inside. There is no entrance fee although visitors need to leave their shoes at the entrance and there is no one to mind them. If this concerns, put them in a bag and carry them with you. Visitors should be respectful about speaking and photography of those praying.

Shalimar Gardens

No one knows where the Shalimar Gardens got their name but they might be named after gardens of the same name built by Emperor Akbar in what is now Indian Kashmir. This garden complex is located about a fifteen minute drive from the Old City along the Grand Trunk Road. It was built by Shah Jahan in the late 1630's to early 1640's. The garden itself is about 40 acres and has three tiers, each descending in height and making use of water brought by a canal. Each of the levels was named (fragrance, bounty, and life) and planted according to the name with a huge number of fruits and flowers. The gardens fell into disuse at the end of the Mughal period and subsequent rulers stripped them of their precious stones and metals. It is believed that during the reign of Ranjit Singh most of the marble was sent to Amritsar for the construction of the Golden Temple. While still impressive in its architecture and design, the waterways and fountains now rarely operate.

Visiting: The complex is open during daylight hours and costs 500 rupees. A ticket booth is located at the main gate.

Dai Anga's Mosque and Gulabi Bagh (Rose Garden) and Dai Anga's Tomb

Dai Anga was the wet nurse of the emperor Shah Jahan, and there are two noted monuments affiliated with her. The first is Dai Anga's mosque, close to Lahore Railway Station, believed to have been built between 1635 and 1639. The mosque sat in what was called Mohalla (community) Dai Anga surrounded by a garden. Other wealthy citizens and members of the Mughal court lived nearby.

Then, half way between Lahore Railway Station and Shalimar Gardens on the Grand Trunk road is the Gulabi Bagh in which Dai Anga's Tomb is found. The garden is home to a beautiful gateway covered in tilework and calligraphy, built around 1655. Dai Anga's tomb, further inside the garden, was likely built around 1671.

Visiting: Both the mosque and the garden are open during daylight hours. There is no fee for visiting either.

Government College

Government College (GC) sits right off Lower Mall Road where it intersects with Mall Road. The college was purpose built at its site between 1872 and 1877 with Lahori brick. Its gothic architecture was likely meant to represent a church and it is easy for the casual observer to mistake it as one. The college was established elsewhere in 1864 and moved to its current site in 1871. It became affiliated with the University of Punjab in 1884 and a university in 2002.

Visiting: The GCU is not open to the public but tourists who wish to visit may contact the administration to arrange a visit. Please visit their webpage for more details: gcu.edu.pk.

Anarkali's Tomb

At the end of Mall road, Anarkali's Tomb is found in an octagonal building which has served as an office, a residence, and a church. It is named after the unfortunate slave-girl Anarkali whose name means 'pomegranate blossom'. She was supposedly a slave girl in the harem of Emperor Akbar and, as the story goes, she fell in love with Prince Salim, who would become Mughal Emperor Jahangir. For this indiscretion, Akbar interred her alive within the tomb.

Modern researchers believe the building to be the tomb of the wife of Emperor Jahangir as there is no evidence to corroborate the story. Despite this a number of plays, songs and even a Bollywood movie have been created about her. Whether the story is true or not, the romantic legend lives on and the neighbourhood is still known by her name.

After the British took up residence in Lahore it was converted into a church and occuped by St. James' Church between 1857 to 1891. Since 1891, the Punjab Archives have occupied the building and now serves as the premises of the Punjab Civil Secretariat and Punjab Records Office.

Visiting: Permission from the Punjab Civil Secretariat must be sought to visit the tomb. The easiest way is to contact a tour guide and ask them to seek permission for you for a specific date and time. During working hours is helpful.

Mall Road (The Mall / Shahrah-e-Quaid-e-Azam)

The Mall, or Mall Road, is one of the best known areas of Lahore as most of the old colonial buildings and parks were constructed along it. Running from just south of the Old City all the way to the Cantonment, it was built to connect the two and named after the British 'Mall' in London. Along the Mall you can find several buildings of both historical and contemporary interest. These are listed in order below, proceeding from the Old City side (Lower Mall) at the General Post Office and on toward the Cantt (Upper Mall).

Traffic along Mall Road can be terrible, especially during rush hours. If you want to take time to observe the buildings the early morning hours on weekends are best. Almost all the buildings on Mall Road are not open to the public and special invitation from each institution is necessary to be allowed entrance.

Town Hall Lahore

The Town Hall is a prominent but unspectacular building housing the Lahore municipality. It was built in 1887 and mainly intended to be used for public functions. After the 1965 Indo-Pak war, the government of Pakistan instructed that special flags be flown to commemorate the support that the people of Lahore, Sialkot and Sargodha gave to the military. These are replaced each year on Defence Day.

Punjab University

The University is the oldest and largest public university in Pakistan and became independent in 1882. It is considered one of the top universities in Pakistan. The university was design by Bhai Ram Singh—a graduate of the National College of Arts and leading architect. He also designed many prominent buildings in Lahore including the Lahore Museum across the street. This is the oldest campus of Punjab University, which has a number of satellite campuses elsewhere.

While there used to be many statues along Mall Road erected in commemoration of various colonial figures only one remains, Alfred Woolner. Woolner's statue keeps its lonely vigil on Mall Road just outside the Punjab University where he served as vice chancellor from 1928-1936.

National College of Arts (NCA)

Originally built in 1875, NCA was originally named the Mayo School of Industrial Arts after a recently assassinated British Viceroy of India. The first principal was Lockwood Kipling, father of author Rudyard Kipling. He was fascinated by local arts and crafts to the extent he insisted that all his students draw the frescos and designs of the Wazir Khan Mosque. The college began to award degrees only in 1985 and became a university in 2011.

Tollinton Market

The market is a long, low, cream coloured building on the same side of the street as the Lahore Museum. It was originally built in 1864 to house the Punjab Exhibition and receive arts and crafts from around Punjab. It then became the Jubilee Museum before the Lahore Museum was built. This is the location that Rudyard Kipling's character Kim describes as 'The Wonder House' when he visits with the Lama. It later became a dry goods market before falling into disuse. Recently as the Lahore City Heritage Museum it opens intermittently to exhibitions such as the Daatchi arts and crafts festivals in April and November.

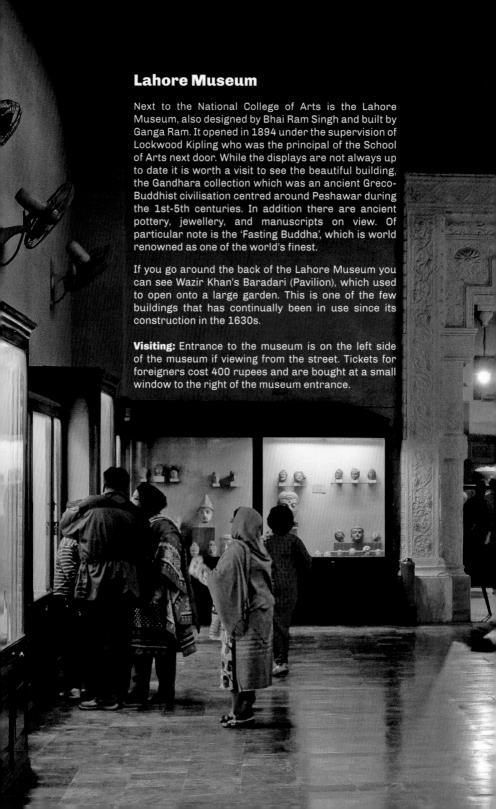

Lahore Museum

Next to the National College of Arts is the Lahore Museum, also designed by Bhai Ram Singh and built by Ganga Ram. It opened in 1894 under the supervision of Lockwood Kipling who was the principal of the School of Arts next door. While the displays are not always up to date it is worth a visit to see the beautiful building, the Gandhara collection which was an ancient Greco-Buddhist civilisation centred around Peshawar during the 1st-5th centuries. In addition there are ancient pottery, jewellery, and manuscripts on view. Of particular note is the 'Fasting Buddha', which is world renowned as one of the world's finest.

If you go around the back of the Lahore Museum you can see Wazir Khan's Baradari (Pavilion), which used to open onto a large garden. This is one of the few buildings that has continually been in use since its construction in the 1630s.

Visiting: Entrance to the museum is on the left side of the museum if viewing from the street. Tickets for foreigners cost 400 rupees and are bought at a small window to the right of the museum entrance.

Zamzama Cannon

Outside of the Lahore Museum in the middle of Mall road sits the 'Zamzama Gun', also known as 'Kim's Gun'.

Zamzama (meaning lion's roar) was made sometime in mid-1700's for Shah Durrani but was damaged and brought to Lahore. It came to be known as 'Kim's Gun' after Rudyard Kipling's character Kim, who played on it in the book, *Kim*:

"He [Kim] sat, in defiance of municipal orders, astride the gun Zam-Zammah on her brick platform opposite the old Ajaib-Gher -- the Wonder House, as the natives call the Lahore Museum. Who hold Zam-Zammah, that 'fire-breathing dragon', hold the Punjab, for the great green-bronze piece is always first of the conqueror's loot."

Anarkali Market & Food Street

Down a side street next to Tollinton Market is the Anarkali food street. This 200-year old market area is believed to be one of the oldest in Asia. It is not to be confused with Anarkali's Tomb which is on the other side Lower Mall Road. Anarkali Food Street is one of the best places to try authentic dhaba (street) food in Lahore. There was another food street, Gawalmandi, nearer to the Old City but this is now open to traffic so less frequented. The only other 'food street' is the line of renovated restaurants overlooking the Badshahi mosque in the Old City.

Most of Mohsin Hamid's book, *The Reluctant Fundamentalist*, is set in this market where Changez and the American stranger have sought out the best cup of tea in Lahore.

Pak Tea House

On the opposite side of the street at the next intersection is the Pak Tea House. Though founded in the 1930's, it only became known as the Pak Tea House after partition in 1947. The cafe was home to youth interested in literature and culture and was associated with the Progressive Writer's Movement. Its central location on Mall Road next to the Oriental College of Punjab University made it a natural gathering point for teachers, authors and poets. It fell into disuse, but was recently opened in 2013 and you can stop in for a cup of tea and moment of inspiration.

Visiting: The Pak Tea House is open 10am to 5pm and never seems to be crowded. If you're a writer you'll find a table with a small plaque reserved for you.

General Post Office

After passing several large banks on both sides of the street, including the Bank of Pakistan, you will see a large, red brick building which is the General Post Office and the largest post office in Pakistan. Its motto? *"Serving everyone, everyday, everywhere"*. It was built in 1887 for the British Queen's Jubilee and designed by Ganga Ram. The post usually works well to/from Pakistan taking only a few days to reach the UK, Europe, and the U.S. Mailing cards and letters only though is advisable to avoid loss or theft of packages.

Eras of Lahore – a cheat sheet

Lahore is so old and the seat of power has transitioned so many times it can be difficult for the average visitor to keep it all straight. Below is a summary of who ruled when, and historical sites associated with their period:

Time period	Ruler	Historic Sites
Pre-history to 1000 AD	Various: Afghan & Rajput rulers	
1022	Ghaznavid Empire: Sultan Mahmud Ghaznavi & Governor Malik Ayaz	Old City Walls (destroyed) Tomb of Malik Ayaz (now reconstructed)
1186	Various Muslim Dynasties including the Delhi Sultanate and First Muslim Sultan: Qutb-ud-din Aibik	Tomb of Qutb-ud-din Aibik (now reconstructed)
1241	Successive Mughal invasions and reigns	
1526	Mughal Empire	Kamran's Baradari (1540)
1556-1608	Mughal Emperor Akbar (the Great)	Lahore Fort (1556)
1605-1627	Mughal Emperor Jahangir	Maryam Zamani's Mosque (1611) Jahangir's Tomb (1637)
1628–1658	Mughal Emperor Shah Jahan	Shalimar Gardens (1630) Dai Anga's Mosque & Gulabi Bagh (1635) Wazir Khan Mosque & Shahi Hamam (1635)
1658–1707	Mughal Emperor Aurangzeb	Chau Burji (late 1600s) Badshahi Mosque (1671)
1707-1799	Chaos: Afghan, Mughal, Maratha & Sikh rule	Golden Mosque (1753)
1799–1839	Sikh Ranjit Singh	Hazuri Bagh & Baradari (1813)
1846–1947	British Raj (rule)	Lahore Railway Station (1859) Lawrence Gardens (1862) Tollinton Museum (1864) Aitchison College (1886) Lahore Zoo (1872) National College of the Arts (1875) Gymkhana Club (1878) Punjab University (1882) General Post Office (1887) Lahore Museum (1894) Lahore High Court (1919) Pak Tea House (1930s) Punjab Assembly (1935)
1947	Partition of India and Pakistan Independence	

Lahore High Court

The court sits on the same side of the street as the GPO and has a large lawn with palm trees in front. The court was first established in 1919 and has jurisdiction over Punjab. The court is well known for the trial of Prime Minister Zulfikar Ali Bhutto which was held there. Bhutto was deposed in a coup in which General Zia-ul-Haq assumed power. The five-month trial resulted in Bhutto being sentenced to death and transferred to Rawalpindi for his execution.

Faisal Chowk (Charing Cross)

After passing several blocks of shopping plazas you will reach Faisal Chowk. It was originally named Charing Cross after the same in London. In the garden is a pavilion in which a statue of Queen Victoria resided until 1951 when it was removed. The pavilion was vacant until 1966 when it was replaced with a bronze Qur'an. The minar (tower) behind it was built in 1974 to commemorate the Islamic Summit held in Lahore as an expression of Muslim solidarity and to discuss the situation in the Middle East after the Arab-Israeli war and oil embargo. The large building behind these two is the Punjab Assembly, built in 1935 to house Punjab's unicameral legislature.

Lahore Zoo

Across from Lahore's large, white Water and Power Authority (WAPDA) building and the Avari Hotel is the Lahore Zoo. Once one of the largest zoos in Asia and believed to be the fourth oldest in the world, it was established in 1872. While not the most modern of zoos it still boasts a huge number of plant, bird and animal life. It is a good outing for children or an afternoon walk.

Visiting: The zoo is open between 9am and sunset.

Lawrence Gardens (Bagh-e-Jinnah)

Adjacent to the Lahore Zoo is a 140-acre park named after John Lawrence, Viceroy of India from 1864-69. The park complex includes the Jinnah (Quaid-e-Azam) Library that is housed in the prominent white colonial building visible from Mall Road, a cricket ground, an open air theatre, tennis court, mosque and botanical gardens. The Jinnah library building used to be known as Montgomery Hall and housed the original Gymkhana Club. The gardens were first planted in 1862 and modelled after Kew Gardens in London. The park contains a huge variety of species of plants and trees which were brought in and raised over time in the gardens. Some of the original plants and trees still have plaques indicating their names. The gardens also contain one of three mounds or hillocks where the British collected the refuse, dirt and debris. All three are visible today, the first being in Lawrence Gardens, the second in Governor's House compound, and the third at the end of Davis Road. The mound in Lawrence Gardens is now covered with vegetation and planted but there are steps leading to the top where there is a better view.

Visiting: The park is open during daylight hours but not before 6am. Entry is free.

Governor's House

On the opposite side of the street from Jinnah Library and Lawrence Gardens is Governor's House. This is a large, white colonial mansion which is the official residence of the Governor of Punjab. The house is built around the tomb of Qasim Khan, the foster brother of Emperor Akbar. The house itself is not visible from the road and the entrance is a heavily guarded brick entry.

Aitchison College

Passing the Pearl Continental Hotel and the government's training college (National Management Institute) you will reach the Aitchison College complex which is behind a long, red brick wall. The college is an elite and prestigious private boys' school built in 1868 as the Punjab Chief's College. It was renamed Aitchison College in 1886 after the Lieutenant Governor of Punjab. Like many of the buildings on the Mall Aitchison was designed by Bhai Ram Singh and built by Ganga Ram.

Visiting: As a functioning school it is not possible to visit and tour the grounds without an appointment. Those interested may contact the school's administration.

Alhamra Art Centre

Directly across the street from Lahore Zoo and next to the Avari Hotel is the Alhamra Art Centre. Run by the Alhamra Arts Council and completed in 1992, the centre has a 450-person theatre and art galleries. Play, festivals, and art exhibitions are held here. It was designed by one of Pakistan's most prominent architects, Nayyar Ali Dada, who also design Qadaffi Stadium in Lahore and Serena Hotel in Islamabad. He won the 1998 Aga Khan Award for Architecture for the building which was called, *"a popular and successful public building projecting its complexities in a simple and powerful manner."*

For information about what is on please visit their website: alhamra.gop.pk/News.php

Gymkhana

The Lahore Gymkhana Club was founded in 1878 for the British who lived in the Cantonment. It is a sports and recreation club offering an 18-hole golf course, squash, swimming, a gym, library, guest rooms and several cafés and restaurants. During the 1965 Indo-Pak war an Indian General famously quipped in a radio address, *"Tomorrow we will drink in Lahore Gymkhana."* Of course, the Indians never made it that far before the war was over. The Gymkhana is a membership club and not open to the public.

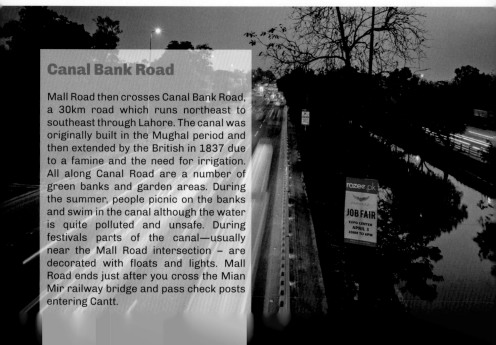

Canal Bank Road

Mall Road then crosses Canal Bank Road, a 30km road which runs northeast to southeast through Lahore. The canal was originally built in the Mughal period and then extended by the British in 1837 due to a famine and the need for irrigation. All along Canal Road are a number of green banks and garden areas. During the summer, people picnic on the banks and swim in the canal although the water is quite polluted and unsafe. During festivals parts of the canal—usually near the Mall Road intersection – are decorated with floats and lights. Mall Road ends just after you cross the Mian Mir railway bridge and pass check posts entering Cantt.

Chau Burji (Four Towers)

Perhaps the most poignant reminder of how modernity and history confront each other is the faded beauty of the Chau Burji. While it used to be the entryway to a massive Mughal garden it now sits unceremoniously in the middle of a traffic island near where the Multan Road (N5) intersects with Jail Road. Originally built in the late 1600s, it was named after a Mughal princess called Zebunisa. Today, busy neighbourhoods and the new Orange Light Rail Line encroach on it but the tilework is still evident and thought to have once covered the entire entrance. One of the minarets collapsed during the British period and was rebuilt between 1973 and 1979.

Visiting: It's possible to just pull over and step out of the car at the Chau Burji but there is no parking available. There is no entrance fee.

Little Shrines Everywhere

All around Lahore are thousands of different shrines dedicated to seemingly unknown persons. These are often decorated with flags, fabric, and tinsel. While some shrines are famous and regularly visited by thousands – such as Data Darbar - most are small, local and unknown. In her book on Lahore, Anna Suvorova calls these 'desi' or 'village', meaning local, shrines. Most often, the shrines are around the tombs of saints (usually Sufi). Some people pray to the saints to grant favour or requests believing that the saint will intercede for them. Some visit to give an offering or make a pilgrimage on the way to an important meeting or trip. Still others simply visit because they are peaceful places for quiet prayer and meditation.

Wagah Border Crossing Ceremony

The Wagah border crossing ceremony is better experienced than described. The ceremony began in 1959 and is performed every day by the Indian and Pakistani military regiments who guard either side of the border. It requires a remarkable amount of coordination between the two country's military which is ironic given that it is, as Michael Palin described, *"carefully choreographed contempt"*. The entire ceremony lasts just under an hour and begins approximately an hour before sundown or at 4pm.

Visiting: There is no entrance fee but it can become quite full, especially on weekends and public holidays. Security was increased with more checkpoints after a nearby suicide bombing in 2014, so it can take some time to reach the border if it's a busy day. The army – who run the event – might note that foreigners are in attendance and question where you are from. Diplomats require protocol in advance to attend.

Tours & Tourism

There are a limited number of tour guides in Lahore. This is likely linked to the limited number of tourists. While it isn't necessary to have a guide as you go about the city, you might feel more comfortable with someone who is knowledgeable about sights. It is possible to pick up a tour guide at many of the larger historical sites—like the Fort and Jahangir's Tomb (or see our recommended guides below). Likewise, the watchmen or gardeners will want to show you around and will be nonplussed that you don't speak any Urdu or Punjabi. A tour of one site should cost no more than 1,000 rupees per person not including entrance fees. However this, like most things in Pakistan, is negotiable. If you work with a tour guide for the full day, it should cost around 5,000 for 1-5 people. A half-day will be around 3,000. Most guides will not have their own transport so will come in your vehicle if you need to move between sites. If you would prefer they can take their own transport just make them aware when you book the tour.

The Tourism Development Corporation of Punjab (TDCP) has a great website for visitors (tdcp.gop.pk) which includes a list of tour operators. In late 2015, the TDCP also started offering sightseeing tours on their two, new, red double-decker, buses. To book a trip, go either to their station right outside the gates of the food street in Heera Mandi (Old City), or contact them via the phone numbers on their website: sightseeing.tdcp.gop.pk.

The Walled City of Lahore Authority (walledcitylahore.gop.pk) is working to preserve and rehabilitate parts of the Old City. They offer four walking tours through the Old City and you can find them at: walledcitylahore.gop.pk. Contact them online or call: +92 (0) 42 992 04237. They also have three 'riding' tours in which you can take your choice of a rickshaw, tonga or buggy ride through the Old City. They are excellent and a fun way to get a sense of the Old City and see the sights.

The Desi Tour Project provides tours in and around Lahore, often in a festively painted and accessorised bus. They have group tours that are very affordable, and aim to encourage Pakistanis to get to know their heritage and culture. Specialised/private tours can also be arranged. Visit their website: desitourproject.com.

Recommended Tour Guides

Imran Ali – Imran is a licensed tour guide and works with the Walled City Authority. He has a website which may be found at: imrantourguide.com.

Peter (Dilawar Masih) – Peter has been giving tours of Lahore for years and has a degree in theology. He may be contacted at: +92 (0) 300 497 3015 or writetopeterm@yahoo.com

Muhammad Javed – Javed is closely affiliated with the Walled City Authority and can often be found at their office in the Delhi Gate of the Old City. His email address is: javedtourlahore@gmail.com and phone number is: +92 (0) 300 435 0693

Sohail Ashraf - Sohail lives in the Old City and knows it well. He can be contacted at +92 (0) 300 483 0982

FOOD & DRINK

Experience the tastes of Lahore

> "Fish need water to breathe, birds need oxygen to survive, Lahoris need food to live. No occasion passes for Lahoris that does not involve food. No conversation ends without mention of food. People go for sehri meals before sunrise in Ramadan: they go to the Walled City at 2:00 a.m. after wedding feasts for food, they plan their lives around dinners, snacks, coffee mornings, breakfasts, brunches, high teas... life in Lahore is one big dinner party and everyone's invited!"
>
> —Sobia Aslam

Any guide to Lahore which didn't spend an inordinate number of pages on food would be remiss. Lahoris devote a huge amount of time and thought to the topic. A true Lahori will begin to think about food the moment they wake up and continue until they go to sleep again. Pakistanis love to talk about food—how best to prepare it, where to find it, and when best to eat it. If you ever find yourself needing to change the subject or wanting to liven up the conversation all you have to do is bring up food. If you love to eat and are adventurous to try new cuisine you will quickly endear yourself to Lahoris.

A Few Food Notes Before You Tuck In

- Almost all Lahori dishes contain meat (usually goat, mutton, chicken or beef) and usually served on the bone. If you're a vegetarian your selection might be limited.
- Go slowly when ordering—each dish ordered in a restaurant is usually enough to serve 3 or 4 people and it is expected that everyone will share the different dishes.
- Lahori food is really rich and usually made with lots of ghee (clarified butter) so there is a layer of oil on top.
- If you don't like spicy (hot) food make sure to let the waiter know. If you like very hot food also let the waiter know as they will often automatically tone down the spice for foreigners.
- People eat with their hands using bread (naan, roti, paratha) to pick up different foods. Using only your right hand is considered polite.
- Pakistani food is a combination of 'dry' (mostly BBQ'ed meats) and 'wet' (curries, dals and other dishes with sauce)—try to order both.
- Meat is served on the bone as a traditional show of wealth. If you'd like something without bones you have to ask for 'boneless' and only a few dishes might be cooked boneless.

What to Eat

If you are new to Pakistan, then start preparing yourself for a feast! Pakistanis love food and Lahoris love food even more. However, if you're not familiar with the names of different dishes the choices for food can be daunting. This section is to help you navigate the menus of Lahore and tell you if there's a particular place renowned for any specific speciality.

Breads

Rice is seldom served as a side dish. Breads, instead, accompany meals including the most common listed below. You'll find all sorts of variations like 'cheese naan' and 'aloo (potato) paratha'.

Roti: The most common bread in Pakistan. It is made of wheat flour and not leavened.

Naan: Unlike Indian naan, Pakistani naan has leaven in it which makes it fluffier and thicker.

Paratha: Mmmm...delicious and heavy—layers of dough usually cooked in ghee (clarified butter).

Biryani / Pilau

Biryani: One of the few times that rice appears in Pakistani cuisine is in biryani. A meal in itself, biryani is rice and a variety of spices such as nutmeg, garlic, coriander, ginger, onions, and lemon, layered with meat (usually beef, chicken, or mutton). It is also usually yellow in colour from saffron (or yellow food colouring).

Pilau: Pilau is also a rice-based dish but it is cooked differently than Biryani. The rice is made from a stock braised with onions and slow-cooked meat on the bone, cinnamon, cardamom and other spices. You can differentiate it from biryani as it tends to be brown in colour instead of yellow.

Alcohol in Lahore

While plenty of Pakistanis partake of alcohol, it is an illegal item for Muslims in Pakistan. This means that there are few places you can go to have a drink, and your selection there will be quite limited. The Avari, Pearl Continental, Holiday Inn, and Ambassador Hotels all have bars for their guests. Foreign brands will be expensive and likely in short supply but if you're looking to try a local brew then ask for a Murree Beer (*murreebrewery.com*).

> "Food is not only an object of gourmandise but also a favourite subject of conversation, somewhat like the weather in England: people speak about what they ate, when and where they ate, and how the food was made."
>
> —Anna Suvorova

Daals (Lentils)

There are a huge number of different dals and dal dishes. Dals come in a variety of colours—green, black, red, yellow—and can be made in a variety of ways and called the same name. So, your Dal Makhani at one place might be completely different from another. Dal is cheap and plentiful and no meal is considered complete without it (and meat).

Chana (or tarka) Dal: This is also known as dal mash or tarka dal. This is a heavy, creamy dal usually made with red or yellow lentils and is super flavourful. Your comfort food of dals. There's a famous restaurant called Mianjee's on the Grand Trunk Road between Lahore and Islamabad that has become famous serving this dish.

Dal Ghost (meat): Usually made with red or yellow lentils, this is like chana dal but with some type of meat - usually goat or mutton.

Dal Makhani: Usually made with black lentils and lots of cream and butter, this is a very rich dal dish.

Haleem: Haleem is made from lentils, barley and wheat which are ground and combined with meat broth to make a thick soup-like dish. While there are lots of places in Lahore that serve haleem, most people will tell you that the home-cooked version is the best. Sprinkle it with fried onions, fresh coriander, ginger, and chilies, and a squeeze of lemon before eating.

BBQ

Now we're getting to the serious business of Punjabi cuisine. Meat. Punjab is renowned for its BBQ'ed (tandoori) meats.

Tikka (chicken, paneer, fish): Anything 'tikka' will usually be a small seasoned cutlet of that item BBQ'ed. Most tikka comes on a skewer kebab style, or on a sizzlingly hot plate.

Kebab (chicken, mutton, beef): Any kebab you order will either be a cut of meat BBQ'ed or that meat ground with spices, formed and then grilled.

Mains Dishes

Chicken chohla: This consists of pieces of chicken cooked slowly for hours with chickpeas. This is a wonderful one-dish meal that makes a change from the normal, Lahori all-meat cuisine. Oh yeah, Lahori's don't consider chicken 'meat'.

Karahi gosht (chicken): Prepared in a large wok (karahi), or a balti, large quantities of diced goat meat are cooked in oil with tomatoes, spices and lots of fresh coriander. You can't go wrong with pretty much any Karahi dish. Locals think that Butt Karahi, just off Laskhmi Chowk serves one of the best in town. Or, try Sarhad's karahi - a dhaba across from Books n Beans near the Pepsi bottler on Gurumangat Road.

Palak Paneer: Not as creamy as the Indian variety palak paneer in Lahore is still cubed cheese (usually fried) and then launched into creamed spinach.

Chicken Handi (boneless): A 'handi' is actually the dish that the food is cooked in so almost anything could be a 'handi'. But the dish that visitors usually know is chicken in a creamy tomato sauce.

Mixed vegetable: Exactly what it sounds like—but be forewarned—the vegetables will usually be boiled/grilled/fried to within an inch of their life!

Rahu: This is a small fish that is usually thickly coated in batter and spices and then fried. When done, the batter is removed to reveal steaming flesh which is then sometimes dipped in a white sauce. On the edge of Model Town is a place called Bashir Darul Mahi that is renowned for their fried fish, as is Siddique's just on Main Blvd.

Nihari: Lahoris claim to do a lot of food better than anyone else but they lay special claim to Nihari. The best places to get it are in the Old City not far from Hathi Gate. Nihari is normally eaten in winter when cuts of beef are cooked slowly overnight in a deep, thick gravy. While previously just a morning treat, it is now served at all mealtimes in other parts of town.

Some well-known mains

If you don't feel like venturing far from the well-known Indian/Pakistan dishes that Westerners are accustomed to then you'll find the following on the menu:

Feeling brave?

We have had all of these and can attest that they're not as unusual tasting as they sound in description. As Lahori specialties we can also guarantee they are delicious.

Thatka-teen (aka thaka-thak or gurda-kapura): The name thaka-thak mimics the sound of a pair of choppers being wielded to dice the food, which includes kidneys, fresh coriander, spices and several pats of butter, with the principal ingredient being goat testicles (or kapuras). Abbot road is known for thatka-thak.

Brain masala: The name pretty much describes it—either cow or sheep brain in a rich, tomato gravy. If you were served it and not told it was brain you would probably never know.

Paya: Also called trotters, which is a more apt description. Trotters have the same status in Lahore's Heera Mandi that onion soup has in Paris's Les Halles district. The legs of mutton are simmered overnight until the marrow is cooked and makes a milky soup. The meat becomes incredibly tender and falls off the bone.

Desserts

While most Pakistanis do have a sweet tooth, the country is not known for its desserts and western-style desserts are served as frequently as Pakistani ones.

Kheer (rice pudding)

Kheer is a sweet, white, rice pudding made of milk, rice, sugar and green cardamom and saffron. It is often served at special occasions and Eid.

Halwa

This heavy paste-like sweet is often made of carrots but can also be made from lentils, pumpkin, or semolina. It is frequently served in a traditional Lahori breakfast.

Sawayan

Served at Eid, this sweet, creamy dish is made of vermicelli with almonds, cardamom and raisins.

Gulab Jaman

Gulab jaman are round balls of donut-like dough made from milk and flour, deep fried and soaked in a cardamom spiced sugar syrup until they become heavy and sweet. They can be eaten hot or cold and are favourites at weddings or in celebration of an event.

Jalebi

Fried jalebis are made by squeezing cursive-like circles of dough through a piping bag into hot oil where they are deep fried. They are then put into sugar syrup and become crispy and chewy. Jalebis are best eaten fresh, hot and crispy from street stalls.

Falooda

Falooda is definitely an acquired taste although Lahoris can't get enough of it. The best way to describe it is as a sweet, milky drink mixed with vermicelli noodles, crushed nuts, and jelly (jello). Almost everyone agrees that the best place to go for Falooda is Riaz's in Anarkali

Kulfi

Kulfi is most often described as being 'South Asian ice cream'. Made from a frozen, cream custard it is dense, rich and normally flavoured with fragrant spices like cardamom, rose and saffron and sometimes incorporates mango and pistachio.

Snacking in Lahore

Lahoris love to snack and throughout the city you'll find people stopping at dhabas and pushcarts day and night to have a snack. Snacks are usually either fruit, or fruit juice, or sugar cane. Roasted nuts and seeds are also a favourite as are deep fried meat or potato samosas. In the winters, roasted corn appears along roadside, and if it rains everyone wants pakora—deep fried vegetables served with yogurt sauce. In a few places, like Liberty Market, you'll find gol gappay vendors (known as pani puri in India—crispy, thin hollow puffs stuffed with a chickpea and potato mixture and a spicy, watery sauce) or chaat, which is chick peas in yogurt and diced onions and tomatoes. If your feeling adventurous and think your stomach can handle it give the street vendors a try!

Where to Eat

Given how much time is devoted to eating in Lahore and how few other social activities there are, going out to restaurants is a main pastime in the city. This means that restaurants do fill up—especially on weekends or during Eid—so consider calling ahead to get a reservation. In general, Lahoris eat late at night so you will find that restaurants will be empty until eight or nine and then packed until midnight. The contact information for restaurants changes often so make sure to check their website or Facebook page for the most updated information.

Restaurants come and go with surprising frequency, so while at the time of writing

these were all current, it is wise to always check before departing. Also make sure to check out the food forums on social media as the food scene is dynamic and there's always a new restaurant opening somewhere.

There are several main eating areas and in each you will find a large number of restaurants including a number not mentioned here.

◆ The Old City—Heera Mandi's Food Street
◆ Gulberg—including M.M. Alam, Qaadafi Stadium, & Liberty Market
◆ Fortress Stadium (Cantonment)
◆ Anarkali Food Street (Mall Road)

The Old City - Heera Mandi's Food Street

If you're looking for authentic Pakistani food with an unparalleled view of Badshahi mosque then head to the food street set on the edge of Lahore's 'red light' district, Heera Mandi. This street is a Lahori landmark with renovated buildings complete with overhanging wooden balconies, hand carved wooden doors and windows, and handmade tiles characteristic of the Old City. You'll notice that some of the restaurants have hanging metal and wood baskets. This is reminiscent of the days when the havelis didn't have kitchens and women were in purdah. The residents would lower money in the baskets and street vendors would send up food from their restaurant kitchens.

Andaaz

andaazrestaurant.com
7pm – 1am
Andaaz has become a Pakistani staple with their flagship restaurant near the Heera Mandi Food Street. Ask to sit on the roof for good views of Badshahi mosque. The menu is authentically Pakistani with a smattering of other South and Central Asian dishes.

Cooco's Den

facebook.com/CoocosDenCafe
5pm – 1am
Cooco's Den is perhaps Lahore's most well-known restaurant. It is owned by Pakistani artist Iqbal Hussain, whose family were 'dancing girls' and worked out of the building he now runs as a restaurant. The restaurant serves Pakistani dishes and is filled with his art capturing the lives of these women and the Heera Mandi neighbourhood. Ask for Table 25 to get the best view of the mosque.

Haveli

haveli.com.pk
6pm -2am
One of the first restaurants on food street, Haveli serves up solid Lahori fare and frequently has live music during dinner. It is also one of the few restaurants with an elevator, so is good for older or disabled visitors. Haveli has a superb view of the mosque with different outdoor levels to dine on. For the best view ask to sit on the very top terrace.

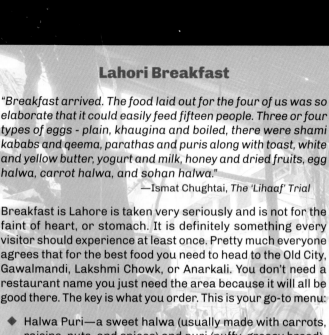

Lahori Breakfast

"Breakfast arrived. The food laid out for the four of us was so elaborate that it could easily feed fifteen people. Three or four types of eggs - plain, khaugina and boiled, there were shami kababs and qeema, parathas and puris along with toast, white and yellow butter, yogurt and milk, honey and dried fruits, egg halwa, carrot halwa, and sohan halwa."

—Ismat Chughtai, *The 'Lihaaf' Trial*

Breakfast is Lahore is taken very seriously and is not for the faint of heart, or stomach. It is definitely something every visitor should experience at least once. Pretty much everyone agrees that for the best food you need to head to the Old City, Gawalmandi, Lakshmi Chowk, or Anarkali. You don't need a restaurant name you just need the area because it will all be good there. The key is what you order. This is your go-to menu:

◆ Halwa Puri—a sweet halwa (usually made with carrots, raisins, nuts, and spices) and puri (puffy, greasy bread)
◆ Nihari—slow-cooked beef or lamb stew
◆ Paya—lamb's legs slow cooked overnight
◆ Channay—chick peas in gravy
◆ Naan / Paratha—the best paratha's are found at Mazang near Qurtaba Chowk
◆ Lassi—a heavy yogurt drink served either sweet or salty

Breakfast timings, like most timings in Lahore, are fluid. Aim for before 1pm. If you don't want to travel all the way to the Old City there are other places to be found like the Capri Restaurant in front of Capri Cinema Lahore in Gulberg with great Lahori breakfast. New food delivery services like www.cheetay.pk will also deliver Lahori breakfast to your house.

Gulberg (including M.M. Alam, Qaadafi Stadium, & Liberty Market)

Gulberg is known for its posh shopping and eateries. There are three main 'areas' where restaurants are clustered in Gulberg – M.M. Alam Road, Qaddafi Stadium and Liberty Market - but sprinkled in between there are some great finds. Restaurants and cafes here tend to be more upscale, Western and trendy, serving continental or oriental fare. A word of warning – while parking in/around Lahore is never easy, finding parking on M.M. Alam in the evenings is near impossible.

Cafe Aylanto
facebook.com/Cafe.Aylanto
Mon-Sat: 12:30 pm - 4:00 pm; 8:00 pm - 12:00 am
Sun:12:30 pm - 4:00 pm; 8:00 pm - 1:00 am
Ask a Lahori about the best place to eat in the city and Café Aylanto will be in the top five. It is one of the places to 'see and be seen' in Lahore. Located on M.M. Alam Road it serves Mediterranean (think: pasta, breads, excellent steaks, creamy desserts) in low-lit indoor and outdoor seating.

Jade Café (by Chinatown restaurant)
facebook.com/Jade-Cafe-by-ChinaTown
Mon – Sun: 8:00am – 1:00am
Great place for breakfast or lunch., Jade Café is still enormously popular a year after opening. You can find it right next to Chinatown restaurant. Skillet omelettes and even blueberry pancakes are on the menu. If you're looking for a great tea selection this is your place.

Qabail
facebook.com/Qabail
A brand new restaurant opened only in 2016 brings you a taste of Pashtun cookery in the heart of Punjab. BBQ'ed meats at their best!

Citrus
facebook.com/citrus.pk
Mon – Sun: 12:00pm – 12:00am
One of the newest additions to the Gulberg Galleria Mall, this is restaurant has a 'fusion' menu so there's lots of variety and as one of the newest restaurants to open it has created a bit of a buzz.

Zucchini
facebook.com/Zucchini-The-Mediterranean-Cafe
Mon – Sun: 12pm – 12am
If there's one mistake many restaurants in Lahore make it's trying to be all things to all people and therefore failing on all fronts. It's difficult to serve every cuisine under the sun and serve it well. Zucchini has avoided this by focusing solely on Mediterranean and Italian foods.

Chinese favourites. You can also order online at their website.

Daar Cheeni
facebook.com/Daar-Cheeni
Mon-Sun: 12pm-4pm; 7pm-12am
Daar Cheeni brings you an Asian/Desi fusion menu with lots of specials that you'll recognise and some that are new and different.

The Lahore Social
facebook.com/thelahoresocial
Now a staple on the Lahore restaurant scene, The Lahore Social is owned by the same proprietor as the Café Upstairs. Although pricey, it is possibly the only place in Lahore where you'll get caramelised pear and rocket salad, salmon sashimi, or pan-seared scallops.

X2 & Desi
x2lahore.com/x2
Monday – Sunday: 11:30am-1:00am
This restaurant complex actually houses three different restaurants in one. If you are looking for Pan-Asian there's X2, if you want Pakistani head upstairs to the outdoor rooftop called Desi. If you want to stop for a quick cup coffee and cake then try their X2 Café.

The Polo Lounge
facebook.com/ThePoloLoungePakistan
The Polo Lounge has long been one of Lahore's upscale restaurants, and is located in the middle of the polo grounds at 'Racecourse' or Jilani Park. It serves burgers, Mongolian chicken, cucumber soup, summer salads, and lamp chop with mint chutney.

Tiramisu
facebook.com/tiramisupakistan
Monday – Sunday: 12.30pm – 12:00am
A seemingly strange combination of Thai, Italian and Continental, this mid-range restaurant is still very popular and known for its chocolate molten cake.

Pompei
facebook.com/pompeilahore
Mon-Sun: 12:30 pm - 3:00 pm; 8:00 pm - 12:00 am
Formerly a favourite only found in Karachi, this upscale restaurant serves up classic Italian fare - pasta, pizza, salads, breads with olive oil and vinegar.

Café Tenerife
facebook.com/TenerifeCafe
Mon – Sun: 12pm – 12am
Located on Jail Road in Gulberg, Café Tenerife serves up Greek, Mediterranean, Middle Eastern, Seafood and Thai. You're bound to find something to make everyone happy.

Ginsoy
facebook.com/Ginsoy; ginsoy.com
Mon – Sun: 12:30pm-3:30pm; 7:30pm–11:30pm
Ginsoy bills itself as 'extreme Chinese' but we found it to have a fairly solid menu of

The Cube Nishat

nishathotels.com/pages/dining/the-cube-29/
In the boutique Nishat Hotel is The Cube a small, upscale restaurant serving Asian fusion as well as high teas in a beautiful, modern interior.

Freddy's Cafe

Well known and right on M.M. Alam Road, Freddy's Cafe is a Lahore staple and does a solid combination of Continental with a little south Asian flare. Good for groups.

Johnny Rockets

.facebook.com/johnnyrockets.pk
Need your fix of 'designer' American fast food and can't bear the thought of McDonald's or Hardees? Then Johnny Rockets is there for you. Burgers, fries, shakes, AND pie. Once deep in DHA and now on MM Alam Road.

Gunsmoke

facebook.com/gunsmokesteakhouse/
If you're looking for huge, good steaks, burgers and chips then this is the place. It's recently moved from M.M. Alam to Gulberg Galleria and its decor is, ahem, decidedly Wild West Americana.

The Cafe Upstairs

facebook.com/thecafeupstairs
Mon – Sun: 8:00am-12:00am
This is described as a bakery-cum-cafe-cum-restaurant with a designated time in-between meals dedicated to the common obsession of Pakistanis—tea. The menu is solidly continental with loads on it, a place where you'll find something for everyone. Also the place if you're looking for breakfast.

Arcadian Cafe

facebook.com/arcadiancafe
Mon-Thurs: 12:30pm – 12:00am
Fri-Sat: 12:30pm – 1:00am
Sun: 1:00pm – 12:00am
We have it on good authority that the Arcadian serves the best chocolate molten lava cake in Lahore—maybe even Pakistan.

English Tea House

facebook.com/EnglishTeaHouseLahore
Mon-Sun: 8:00am – 12:00am
Tucked away behind YUM, right off M.M. Alam is the English Tea House modelled on, you guessed it, an English Tea House. Lunch or high tea here are the order of the day. Cakes are very good. They also have another branch in DHA 3.

Tokyo

facebook.com/TokyoPakistan
Don't know what Teppanyaki is? Well, let this restaurant introduce you to Japanese grilling where the chef cooks right before you. It also has quality sushi and tends to be slightly easier on the wallet than the restaurants in the Avari.

Cosa Nostra

facebook.com/Cosa-Nostra-Lahore
Tucked down a side street, Cosa Nostra is reputed to have the best thin-crust pizza in the city. The gelato made on site is definitely worth a stop and they also provide it in quarts for take away.

YUM

yumpakistan.pk
Mon – Sun: 12:00pm – 4:00pm; 7:00pm – 12:00am
There is consensus that there is no truly great Chinese food in Lahore but this one is a solid second and easier on the wallet than Dynasty.

The Delicatessen & The Pantry

facebook.com/TheDelicatessenByCosaNostra
Mon-Sun: 11am – 10pm
facebook.com/ThePantrybyTPL
Mon-Sun: 10am-10:30pm
If one good turn deserves another this is

what Cosa Nostra and The Polo Lounge have decided to do by putting two, virtually identical, cafes next to each other in Gulberg. Both serve good coffees and drinks with light lunch fare, cakes and sweets. Both have a good bread section and baked goods for eating in or taking away.

Mocca Coffee
facebook.com/moccacoffee
And, right next to The Delicatessen & The Pantry is Mocca with its clean, modern interior, coffee, cakes and even some gluten-free desserts.

Café Barbera
facebook.com/CafeBarberapk
Mon – Thurs: 8:00am – 1:00am
Fri – Sat: 8:00am – 2:00am
Sun: 9:00am – 1:00am
Amongst a sea of restaurants and cafes that open at noon, Café Barbera's 8am opening is positively refreshing for all (both?) of the morning people in Lahore. Serving up coffees and café food it is especially renowned for its breakfasts.

Coffee Tea & Company
Reputedly has a very good breakfast and is a good place for both coffee, and surprise, tea.

The Lebanese Lounge
lebaneselounge.com.pk
There are only a few places that do justice to Mediterranean cuisine and this is one of them. Lebanese favourites are served under a large, outdoor atrium. Here's where you

can get your hummus, baba ganoush, shish taouk and tabouleh.

Café Zouk
facebook.com/CafeZoukLahore
Café Zouk has been around for 21 years, which is far longer than most other restaurants so they must be doing something right. Serves continental and Asian.

Byrggen
facebook.com/Bryggen.Pk
Mon-Sun: 12:00pm – 11:30pm
Byrggen made a splash on the Lahore culinary scene when it opened in 2015 serving European and Norwegian food right on MM Alam Road.

Spice Bazaar
facebook.com/spicebazaarpk
Spice Bazaar is the latest venture of YUM and the English Tea House but focuses entirely on Pakistani (desi) and Afghani cuisine. It gets good ratings for both its ambience and service.

Monal
lahore.themonal.com
facebook.com/monallahore
Mon – Sun: 11:00am – 12:00am
Monal made waves when they opened a restaurant high atop the Margalla hills in Islamabad. Attempting to replicate that success they opened a restaurant in Lahore high atop...a parking garage in Liberty Market. How patrons feel about the food tends to reflect how they feel about the view—which is much higher than any of the surrounds.

Scafa
facebook.com/pages/Scafa-the-School-of-Culinary-and-Finishing-Arts-Lahore
On the ground floor of the EFU building this is a fine dining experience you'll get nowhere else in Lahore. Every night they serve a seven course meal to between 10-15 guests. Meals are prepared by foreign and Pakistani chefs as well as the students studying culinary arts at the school. A reservation is a MUST!

Bundu Khan
bundukhan.pk
Mon – Sun: 12:00pm – 1:00am
If you're out shopping and want authentic

Pakistani food without the high prices and formality of Heera Mandi, then try Bundu Khan. This Lahori institution has 10 restaurants in the city but those likely to be closest to where you are will be the locations at Liberty Market, Fortress Stadium, or DHA.

Qaddafi Stadium

Qaddafi Stadium is the cricket stadium in Lahore and around its exterior base are any number of very good restaurants. We recommend only a few here.

Dera & Dhaba

Little known outside Lahori circles the 'Dera Restaurant' is located outside Qadaafi Stadium. Here you'll find the quality of Pakistani food normally reserved for the Old City but without having to navigate Old City crowds and traffic.

Buzkash Restaurant

facebook.com/buzkash.lhr
Buzkash serves up Central Asian food with a particular emphasis on Afghani cuisine. Definitely worth a try. (Misspell Buzkash on google and you'll get Buzkashi which literally means, 'goat dragging' and is a Central Asian sport where riders drag a goat or calf carcass toward the opponent's goal)

Defence Housing Authority (DHA)

Mouthful

facebook.com/mouthful.pk
Best described as Pakistani / Continental fusion this restaurant has beer can chicken, tandoori chicken wings, and philly cheesesteak. Self-described as a healthy option with organic eggs and meat, no microwaves, deep-frying, or msg.

Johnny & Jugnu

facebook.com/Johnnyandjugnu/
Simple burgers and wraps with a twist in that the proprietors are convinced that the seven sauces they use make their burgers and wraps a step above the rest. There is no seating but the limited menu is a refreshing change and means they are perfecting what they make!

Maro Tandoors

facebook.com/marotandoors
marotandoors.com
Four friends at LUMS decided to start a little naan shop putting cheese, pizza, meat, and most famously, Nutella in naans. Their original shop is in Model Town but now they have an 'upscale' version in DHA. In 2016, to mock the Lawn fabric fashion craze/season they launched a 'Nawn' collection.

Mall Road & surrounds

Mall Road itself doesn't have many restaurants but step down some side streets and there's plenty to be found.

Lasksmi Chowk

At the junction where at Abbot and McLeod roads meet you'll find Lakshmi Chowk. Not so much a restaurant as an area where you can find amazing street food. Step down a side street and you'll find restaurants and street dhabas that never seem to close. The Butt name is prominent here (which never ceases to get a giggle) with Butt Karahi being exceptionally well known, as is Butt Sweets and Bakers

Fujiyama

avari.com/property/avari-lahore/dining/fujiyama
Mon – Sun: 12:00pm – 3:30pm; 7:00pm – 11:30pm
Better known as the 'Japanese restaurant in the Avari Hotel' there are two Teppanyaki counters where the chefs slice, dice and cook in front of you. Comes with a hefty price tag but sometimes you just need sushi.

Dynasty

avari.com/property/avari-lahore/dining/dynasty
Mon – Sun: 12:00pm – 3:30pm; 7:00pm – 11:30pm
Dynasty gets mixed reviews but if you want Szechuan Chinese, dim sum, or Cantonese in Lahore, this is the place. Also in the Avari Hotel.

L'Auberge

falettishotel.com/restaurants_lebanese.php
The best Middle Eastern cuisine in Lahore does not come cheap but if you are looking for some authentic Lebanese food then you have to visit L'Auberge in the beautiful Faletti's Hotel.

Other areas
Anarkali Food Street

At least 200 years old, Anarkali is one of the oldest surviving markets in Asia and derives its name from a nearby mausoleum thought to be that of a slave girl named Anarkali who was buried alive by order of the Mughal Emperor Akbar for the indiscretion of having an affair with his son and heir. If you're looking for the Pakistani street food experience this is the place, but while the food is delicious, the place can be crowded, hot and definitely not high end. In 2013, there was either an IED attack or gas canister explosion here, which puts it on the no-go list for some.

Gawalmandi Food Street

Near the Anarkali neighbourhood is Gawalmandi food street which used to have a diverse selection of street food as families moving to Lahore after partition settled there bringing their different dishes and cooking techniques with them. The street was open only to foot traffic and the facades of buildings painted and lit. It fell prey, however, to politics

and a change in government meant it was opened up again to traffic which reduced patronage. The street is still worth a visit as it serves up some of the best street food in Lahore but outdoor seating is limited.

Peeru's Café
facebook.com/Peerus.Cafe
Mon – Sun: 1:00pm – 12:00am
Great for a cultural night out, this beautiful café complex has an atmospheric courtyard and also houses a museum of puppetry. There is live traditional music (sufi qawwali and ghazals) on Thursday, Friday and Saturday nights. The location is a little far out on Raiwind road and can be confusing to get to, so make sure you/your driver has good directions beforehand.

Food Truck Company
facebook.com/ftcpakistan
Mon-Thu & Sun: 4:00pm – 12:00am
Fri – Sat: 4:00pm – 1:00am
Did you come to Pakistan thinking you could escape the hipsters? No such luck. There are food trucks even here. FTC is around Lahore daily serving up burgers, fries and shakes. Check their Facebook page each day to find out where they'll be—or their home page also shows the location of the truck at any given time.

Loca
facebook.com/LocaLahore
While it's not entirely authentic Mexican or South American, Loca gets credit for being the next closest thing in Lahore. They've taken their restaurant on the road and now have a food truck—on Thursday and Fridays are near Kalma Chowk. Check out their Facebook to find out where they are the rest of the time.

Lahorelicious
web.facebook.com/lahorelicious
Artisan, handcrafted ice cream from rBGH free milk, free range egg yolks, imported vanilla, swiss chocolate and fresh seasonal fruits making flavours like Salted Butter Caramel, Mint & Lindt, and Vanilla Oreo. This ice cream business delivers directly to you - just order through cheetay.pk or on their facebook page.

Madagascar Vanilla

Salted Butter Caramel

Chocolate Fudge Brownie

Strawberry Cheesecake

Online Food Forums

At a loss as to which restaurant to choose? Looking for some specific cuisine in Lahore? Just want to spend some time thinking and discussing Pakistani dishes? Then join one of the Food Forum Facebook groups devoted to food in Lahore. They will give tips and points for practically any food related question you have in Lahore.

◆ Foodies R Us: web.facebook.com/Foodies-R-Us
◆ Foodies Lahore: facebook.com/foodies.lahore
◆ Lahore Food Forum: facebook.com/groups

Also, if you just want to read about different restaurants try: www.paitbhar.com.

Food Delivery

Lahoris love to eat so much that they have multiple ways of ensuring that they never have to go out (or cook). There are a number of delivery services in Lahore that will bring food to you pretty much anywhere.

◆ Cheetay: Delivers food from any restaurant in Lahore to anywhere in Lahore. *cheetay.pk*
◆ Food Panda & Eat Oye: Just register at either *foodpanda.pk* or *eatoye.pk*, put in your delivery address and different restaurants menus available for order will turn up.
◆ ShutUp and Eat: *facebook.com/ShutUpAndEatPk*
◆ Midnight Munchies: A delivery and takeaway that only works from 8pm to 3am (4am on Thurs-Sat) *facebook.com/midnightmunchiespk*.

Lahore Eat Food Festival

It goes without saying that a city that loves food as much as Lahore would have its own food festival. And Lahore does. Lahore Eat launched in February 2016 with a three day event in Jillani Park. In addition to a great variety of food to taste there are also talks, competitions, exhibitions, demonstrations by celebrity chefs, band performances, and games for kids. It is planned to be an annual event

Too Much Choice?

"The Lahoris loved food. They did not believe in 'eating to live'. They would go to any length to gratify the cravings of their palates as much as the demands of their stomachs, and often much beyond."

—Pran Nevile

Lahori foodies have made complaining about food and service an art form (check out the food forums) but the one complaint they would not have is that they're spoiled for choice. However, if you're here on a short visit it's easy to be overwhelmed. Here's a short list to help:

◆ Authentic Pakistani with ambience? Try Andaaz, Haveli, or Cooco's Den on the food street in the Old City.
◆ Modern Pakistani? Try Desi at X2 or Spice Bazaar
◆ Somewhere with something for everyone? Café Aylanto
◆ Breakfast? Amu (Fri-Sun only)
◆ Lunch? The Delicatessen, The Pantry, or the Café Upstairs
◆ Asian? Upscale – Fujiyama or Dynasty; Moderate - Ginsoy
◆ Ice cream? Gelato at Cosa Nostra or Lahorelicious (home delivery)
◆ Something different? Book at SCAFA, this culinary school and restaurant will not disappoint. Tasting menu only with 2 seatings at 8pm and 10pm.

Add a little spice to your life...

If you love to cook then Lahore is the city for you. The city's markets and roadside stalls are filled with fresh fruit and vegetables. Some that you'll have heard of and some that will be new. Spices are plentiful and getting to know them is a delight for any cook. Fruit tends to come in waves from all over the country as the seasons change - mangos, strawberries, watermelon, peaches, oranges... the list goes on. Lahore has also begun to embrace clean and healthy eating with local and organic products being sold at specialty markets (such as Khalis Food Market – khalisfoodmarket.com) or by Pakistan brands like Daali Earth Foods which can be found in some grocery stores.

Move Over Chef Zakir

"Think of the Rao fish at Bhati Gate, or the naan-kebab from Dar-ul-Kabab situated to the left of Mozang Chungi, remember the vats of nihari breakfasts in the old city, and the glorious degh filled with a most elegant halim."

—Sara Suleri Goodyear, *Lahore Remembered*

Muhammad Zakir Qureshi is a popular Pakistani chef who stars in television shows about Pakistani cooking. But you don't need years of training to impress your friends and family when you return home and whip up some Pakistani grub. Despite the complex nature of spices and length of time involved in cooking Pakistani food, you'll easily be able to replicate a couple of dishes in your own kitchen. Below are two recommended for amateur chefs...

Chicken Karahi (wok) – a simple and flavourful chicken dish
1. Cut between 2-4 chicken breast (boneless) into small cubes
2. Dice a small onion
3. Peel, then dice a 'thumb' (2 tbsp) of ginger
4. Peel, then dice three cloves of garlic
5. Dice 3-4 tomatoes
6. Chop a handful of fresh coriander (cilantro).
7. Put the onion, ginger, and garlic in a blender or food processor and make into a paste. Add a tsp of water if necessary.
8. Put 8 tbsp butter in a frying pan and heat. Add the onion/garlic paste to the frying pan and heat for 1-2 minutes.
9. Add 1 tsp ground coriander, 1 tsp cumin, 1 tsp chili powder, 1 tsp allspice to the frying paste. Let simmer for 1-2 minutes.
10. Add the chopped tomatoes. Let the tomatoes cook and their water evaporate until it makes a thick sauce. Turn down to avoid burning.
11. Add the chicken to the frying pan and coat with the sauce. Cook for 10 minutes or until the chicken is done.
12. Add the chopped coriander and serve with rice, naan, or roti.

Tarka Dal – a nice, simple red, or yellow, dal dish with just the right amount of spice
1. Peel and dice one onion
2. Peel and dice 3 garlic cloves (keep 2 of diced cloves separate)
3. Peel and dice 1 tbsp (1 thumb) fresh ginger
4. Melt 2 tbsp butter in a deep pan or pot over medium heat
5. Add the onions, 1 diced garlic clove, and ginger. Cook for 4-5 minutes stirring to avoid burning.
6. Add 2 cups of red (or yellow) lentils, ½ tsp turmeric, and four cups of water
7. Bring to a boil and then turn down heat to medium. Allow the lentils to cook until they have thickened and absorbed the water – usually 45 minutes.
8. In a small frying pan put 1 tbsp butter, ½ tsp chili flakes, ½ tsp fennel seeds, ½ tsp cumin seeds, 2 bay leaves and the remaining 2 cloves of diced garlic.
9. Heat slowly and stir to release the aroma of the spices taking care to not allow it to boil or burn.
10. Add to the lentils and serve immediately

SHOPPING
Shop 'til you drop

There is no comprehensive shopping guide to Lahore but there is plenty of shopping! It's a great adventure to plunge into the markets of the Old City or pick a shopping centre – there is one on virtually every corner – and explore the different shops in it. While there are shops sprinkled throughout Lahore there are several shopping 'hubs' or neighbourhoods in which good shopping is clustered. Of course, what you want to buy will dictate where you will go, but a description of some of the prominent shopping areas are described below.

When planning your shopping do not schedule an early start. Shops open sometime between 10 and noon and stay open until between 10 and midnight. Take your time, sleep late and have a leisurely breakfast before you head out. Also, most shops will be closed for Juma (longer, weekly prayers) on Fridays between 12 and 4pm.

If you're interested in buying women's clothing, you'll need to decode a few terms. First, there are two 'seasons' or lines of clothing that most fashion houses produce: lawn (summer) and cambric (winter). Lawn is also a fine weave of fabric made out of either cotton or linen or a mixture of the two. Clothes come in 'pret' or ready-made, or unstitched, meaning that you buy fabric and take it to a tailor to have it made up.

If you're looking for bargains make sure to

take advantage of the sales. Toward the end of the lawn season (August) and the end of the winter season (January) retailers will massively discount their products from 30-70%. Beware though, sale days are madness and incredibly crowded with plenty of pushing and shoving so put your game face on and be prepared!

For information about when to haggle and when prices are fixed see page 28.

Shopping Areas

Gulberg - M.M. Alam Road
Named after a famous Pakistani fighter pilot, Muhammad Mahmood Alam, this street and its immediate surrounds is Lahore's best known shopping area. Here you'll find most of the big-name, high-end shops and a large number of well-known restaurants. If you're looking for 'desi' (Pakistani) clothes, or even western-styled clothes by Pakistani designers, M.M. Alam is a good place to start.

Gulberg Galleria
gulberggalleria.com
The Gulberg Galleria is a new mall that opened in 2015 with plenty of the the names you expect to see like Nishat Linen, Hopscotch, but also Elan and Muse. It also contains a number of good cafes and restaurants like Delish, Mocca, GunSmoke and Cold Stone.

Gulberg - Liberty Market

Liberty Market is a huge complex of shops and shopping centres built in a concentric horseshoe shape. Here you'll find more shops than you could possibly ever visit, selling clothing, home wares, fabric, shoes, jewellery and children's toys.

Cantonment - Mall of Lahore

malloflahore.pk

This is the best known shopping mall in Lahore, but bear in mind it's in the Cantt so foreigners might have difficulty accessing it. While Pakistan is still lacking some of the big name brands you'll find in Dubai, London or New York, it still has a fairly good selection. Names like Accessorize, Body Shop, Limelight and Adidas will be here.

Additionally, the giant household and grocery store HyperStar (owned by Carrefour) has a branch in Cantt.

Cantonment - Fortress Stadium

If you're after an authentic Pakistani shopping experience, this is the place to go. Surrounding the stadium are lots of shops selling clothes, fabric, shoes and other accessories. Immediately adjacent to the shopping area you'll also find Fortress Square Mall (fortresssquare.com)

Defence Housing Authority (DHA)

Almost all shops that are to found on M.M. Alam or Gulberg also have locations in DHA. DHA is laid out in blocks and the best shopping is in Y and Z blocks.

New Malls

In addition to the areas above two new, large malls are planned in Lahore with openings in 2017. The first is the Emporium Mall by the Nishat Group near the Lahore Expo Centre (nishatemporium.com). The second is the Packages Mall (mall.apponative. com/) near Model Town off Ferozpur Road. Both these malls will be out of areas frequently visited by visitors but will be worth the trip.

Products

Online

Pakistan is a relative late-comer to online shopping but it's now catching on. If you're looking for handicrafts and other quality products from Pakistan you won't find many through major online retailers (like Amazon). However, a couple of websites have been recently established which you might enjoy and there will certainly be more to come!

Polly and Other Stories

pollyandotherstories.com
Following the popularity of the Pakistani brand Polly & Me's purses and bags comes Polly and Other Stories, "Pakistan's FIRST online store for hand-made, unique products sourced from the region, giving big voices to little ventures." Think of it like the Etsy of Pakistan.

Chamki Truck Art & Décor

facebook.com/ChamkiTruckArtDecor
If you love Pakistani truck art and would like a home décor piece made or personalised check out Chamki's line.

Shubinak

shubinak.com
A fun Pakistani clothing and home décor brand that aims to both reflect the culture as well as follow eco-friendly and sustainable practices.

BISP E-Commerce

yayvo.com/home-decor/handicrafts/arts-craft/ahan.html
The name certainly doesn't tell the whole story. This site was an initiative of the Government of Pakistan's Benazir Income Support Programme. It provides support to some 5.2 million of the poorest women in Pakistan. Those who receive quarterly cash stipends are allowed to market their products here, giving them a chance to supplement their incomes.

9Lines

9lines.net
A 'quirky fashion, art and lifestyle brand'. On 9Lines you'll find the work of artist Hassan Iqbal Rizvi on clothes, accessories and items for the home. If you're looking for a fun gift from Pakistan for a younger person you'll definitely find it here.

Clothing

Only a selection of the major retailers are listed here. There are *hundreds* of other fashion studios and clothing stores in Lahore and everyone has a favourite.

Al Karam

alkaramstudio.com/pk
A textile company founded in the 1980's, Al Karam Studio – which carries their women's line – has three stores in Lahore. One in Gulberg on the Main Boulevard, one in DHA Y Block, and one in Liberty Market.

What to buy in Pakistan (and what not to!)

Shopping in Pakistan is an absolute pleasure. As historic middlemen on ancient trading routes, Pakistanis have perfected the ability to produce beautiful and artistic goods and if they don't produce it they can certainly get it for you. This doesn't mean, however, that everything is a good deal. Much of what is on offer will be imported and it is essential to buy local to get the best deal.

Buy:

Carpets
Pakistan has a long tradition of carpet weaving dating back to before the Mughal rule. Some of the first 'oriental' carpets introduced to Europe came from Lahore. Today, hand woven carpets are one of Pakistan's largest industries and almost all carpets are produced for export. Take care however, as much of what is sold as 'hand woven' is actually machine made. Also, the working conditions of labourers in the carpet industry can be terrible. Try to get to know a carpet dealer like Bunyaad (see page ?) and buy fair trade.

Jeans
Given the amount and type of cotton grown in Pakistan, the country is one of the largest producers of denim globally. This means that denim products – including jeans – tend to be much cheaper here than abroad.

Leather products
If you ever wanted a bespoke pair of leather brogues, boots, or a purse or wallet Pakistan produces a lot of leather products. Many leather shops can even make products based on a picture shown to them.

Semi-precious stones
The mountain ranges in the north of Pakistan along the border with Afghanistan make Pakistan a leader in gemstone mining and production. Some gemstones which are mined in Pakistan are: aquamarine and topaz (both from Shigar Valley in Gilgit-Baltistan), emeralds (from Swat Valley in Khyber Pakhtunkhwa), garnet, peridot and quartz (from northern Pakistan), rubies (from Kashmir), and lapis lazuli and amethyst (from Aghanistan).

Fabrics, scarves & blankets
Pakistan is known for its fabrics including beautiful prints, and beautifully embroidered and printed scarves and blankets. This includes the wool blankets known in the Pashtun areas as well as Kashmiri, Pashmina, and Indian shawls.

Art & Framing
Pakistani artists are on the rise in the global art world but remain relatively unknown. Now is the time to invest in a piece of art that you love. Frames in Pakistan are made to order and a piece of poster-sized art with matting and glass may cost as little as $60-$80 USD.

Don't Buy:

Diamonds & Gold
This is not strictly true. Diamonds and gold may be bought in Pakistan and their prices can be far less than can be found in Europe. However, they are not produced here and their price will reflect global market value.

Antiques
Again, not strictly true but visitor Pakistan and being offered antiques should be wary of their true age. There are real great antiques in Lahore but you need to delve into the recesses of markets for them.

Western Goods
Because few western name brands are in Pakistan imports are reflected in the price the customer pays.

Fakes
Knock-off and look-alike products are everywhere in Pakistan. From watches, to purses, to DVDs. Pakistan has loose copyright and patent enforcement but the country you're coming from might not look so kindly on you returning with fakes.

BeechTree

beechtree.pk
Consisting entirely of pret / ready made clothing, Beechtree carries more trendy clothes with a lower price tag that younger people will appreciate. They have five shops in Lahore, one each in: Liberty Market, DHA, Gulberg, on M.M. Alam, and DHA.

FashionCentral

facebook.com/fashioncentralpk
Primarily known as a fashion magazine, Fashion Central also has a multi-brand store on M.M. Alam Road where some well-known (and some lesser known) designers sell their brands. It's located right above Butler's Chocolate Café.

Generation

generation.com.pk
Starting in the mid-1980's, Generation has become a well-loved staple on the fashion scene. Their store in Lahore is right near Main Market at the north of M.M. Alam Road.

Hopscotch

ilovehopscotch.com
Founded by a Lahori couple, Hopscotch has become the foremost name in children's clothing in Pakistan. They carry clothes for kids aged 0-12 and have four locations in Lahore: Gulberg Galleria, DHA, Mall of Lahore and a Factory Outlet in Al Karim Mall

Ideas by Gul Ahmed

ideas.com.pk
The Gul Ahmed name has been dealing in textiles and clothing in Pakistan since the early 1900s. The brand has several stores —some located as a department within other shops—in Lahore, but the two in Gulberg are in Main Market and Liberty.

Khaadi

khaadionline.com/home.php
An extremely popular clothing store in Pakistan and internationally. Khaadi opened in 1998 and has seven stores in Lahore with its flagship store being on the corner of College Road and M.M. Alam.

Limelight

limelight.pk
facebook.com/limelight.pret
Limelight established stores in 2010 and its flagship store is right on M.M. Alam. They carry exclusively pret / readymade clothing and accessories. Their prices tend to be cheaper than some of the other brands.

Sana Safinaz

sanasafinaz.com
Started by two friends (Sana & Safinaz) in 1989, this is one of the most prominent Pakistan fashion houses. While Sana Safinaz has three stores in Lahore (one in Gulberg Galleria and one in DHA) you'll find this store right at the end of M.M. Alam just across Ali Zaib Road.

Sapphire

facebook.com/sapphireofficial
Although an established textile company, Sapphire is a relative newcomer to the retail scene, establishing a store in Lahore in 2014. It is right on the corner of Sir Syed Road and College Road.

Photo courtesy of House of Kamiar Rokni

Suits, Tailoring & Luxury Wear

If you ever wonder why your colleagues and friends in Pakistan seem incredibly well turned out it's because most of their clothes are tailored for them. Most people don't buy ready-made clothes but select fabric, visit a tailor and have them made.

Men's Tailoring

If you're looking for a middle-range suit or shalwar kameez try Dandy (*dandydesigns. pk*). They have locations on both Mall Road as well as M.M. Alam. Depending on the fabric, and type of suit, a bespoke suit will cost in the range of $200-$500 USD. Collared men's business shirts will cost in the range of $20-$30, again depending on the style and fabric.

For a special occasion, or a higher end suit, go to Rici Melion and see Noman who has a big, new shop on M.M. Alam. You'll have several fittings but your suit will be top notch. You can see some recent suits here: *facebook.com/ricimelion* as well as on Instagram.

Women's Luxury Wear & Tailoring

If you've bought an unstitched Pakistani suit from a high street shop you have a few options to get it tailored for you. The first is to check with the shop. Some will either have a tailor in house who can measure and make it for you or some will give recommendations of women's tailors with whom they work. A number of women's tailors are also located along M.M. Alam and in Main Market.

If you're looking for a keepsake piece of luxury Eastern wear you should try:

House of Kamiar Rokni

facebook.com/TheHouseOfKamiarRokni
Inspired by Pakistan's cultural heritage and its modern aesthetic interpretation, the House of Kamiar Rokni is known for its luxury bridal wear and haute couture often seen on the fashion runways, in the Sunday magazines, and on celebrities.

Rano's Heirlooms

facebook.com/ranosheirlooms
With a store on Main Blvd in Gulberg, Rano's Heirlooms specialises in luxury and bridal wear

If you're looking for a piece of luxury Western wear you should try:

House of Latif

facebook.com/houseoflatif
House of Latif has two lines: Zuria Dor which is their evening wear and Daria Enzo which is their day wear. The pictures don't do their beading and finishing work justice. It's incredibly intricate and well done. Also, it's all made-to-measure so reduces the impact of high fashion on the environment. They deliver to your door worldwide and their dresses have already been worn at award shows in London including Sheridan Smith's dress at the 2016 BAFTAs and Isobelle Molloy at London Fashion Week. Check out their Instagram for lots more photos: zuriador.

GROCERY / DEPARTMENT STORES

For fresh produce most people visit the open air markets where fruits and vegetables are plentiful and cheap. However, a smaller selection can be found in some grocery stores. The same goes for meat which many people buy from a butcher. Dry goods and household items are the main items in these grocery / department stores listed.

Al Fatah
alfatah.pk
Al Fatah is perfect for grocery or household shopping. They have several stores in Lahore —one in DHA and a new, large department store on Mian Mehmood Ali Kasoori Rd in Gulberg.

Green Valley
greenvalley.pk
Green Valley is a department store popular with foreigners as it stocks a wide range of foreign products and tends to be clean, well-ordered and not as crowded as some other stores. It also has a wide meat and vegetable selection with imported items. Unfortunately, it is in Cantt and foreigners might have difficulty accessing.

Hyperstar
facebook.com/hyperstar.pakistan
Think Walmart or a giant Tesco, and you'll envision Hyperstar which is owned by Carrefour. They have appliances, household items, clothing and groceries. Unfortunately, it is also in Cantt and foreigners might have difficulty accessing.

Jalal & Sons
jalalsons.com.pk
Established in 1948, Jalal & Sons is a household name and your local grocery. It won't have a lot of the imported goods as other stores but does have a wide range of food and items. They have outlets throughout Lahore

Metro
metro.pk
The closest thing Pakistan has to a big lot, membership store Metro has two locations in Lahore. One in Model Town and one on Ravi Road near the Old City. Great if you're looking to buy in bulk.

BOOKSTORES

There are a large number of bookstores in Lahore which carry either books in Urdu and other local languages, or a mix of these and English. The following are bookstores that carry predominantly English language works.

The Last Word
facebook.com/TheLastWordbks/
Missing your independent bookstore from back home? This great little bookstore will remind you of it. Right above the Lahore Social restaurant on M.M. Alam Road. It will have the latest releases as well as classics, and an eclectic mix in between. They hold book events and readings and a regular Saturday morning book reading for kids.

Readings

readings.com.pk

Like many things in Lahore this bookstore doesn't look like much from the outside, but inside you'll a huge variety of books and they also have a tremendous selection online and have free home/cash on delivery in Lahore. The store is right on Gulberg Main Blvd, not far from M.M. Alam Road and Main Market.

Liberty Books

libertybooks.com

Liberty books has an enormous online selection as well as bookstores in the Mall of Lahore, Avari Hotel and in the Hyperstar department stores.

Books and Beans

facebook.com/ booksnbeanss

Tucked away near the Pepsi bottler in Gulberg is Books and Beans. They have a good selection of English language books as well as a small cafe. (Across the street you'll find one of the best karahi dhabas in Lahore)

Sang-e-Meel Publications

sangemeel.com

Looking for some interesting reading on

Pakistan or South Asia? Sang-e-Meel carries titles you'll only find in Pakistan. They publish a number of prominent Lahori writers and historians. They have a shop on Lower Mall Road.

Variety Books

varietybooks.com.pk

Located at the edge of Liberty Market on Noor Jehan Road, Variety has a good stock of English language books as well as stationery, wrapping, papers, and cards.

Ferozsons

ferozsons.com.pk

Another big book distributor and bookstore is Ferozsons which sells books both online as well as from their location on Mall Road.

HANDICRAFTS

While Pakistan produces a huge amount of local handicrafts (such as Multan pottery, brassworks, marble & wood carvings, shawls, woollen wraps, etc.), there is no collection of handicraft stores in any one location in Lahore. A couple of times a year, usually in November and April, the Daachi Foundation (*daachifoundation.org*) holds an Arts and Crafts Fair in the Tollinton Museum on Mall Road, bringing together local artists and NGOs who exhibit their crafts. They are also planning an 'Artisans Village' in Raiwind which could host these artists and groups on a more regular basis, but this has yet to open. In the meantime, a small number of stores are listed here:

Shawls/Wraps

For a good selection of different shawls and wraps (silk, Kashmir, Pashtun) best to scour the small shops in either Liberty or Fortress Stadium markets.

Carpets & Jewellery

Pakistan is a great place to buy both. However, as you're likely not an expert on these it's easy to be decieved. Most visitors can't tell the difference between a machine or hand-knotted carpet, or between a treated or untreated ruby. While most crafts people are honest we can only, in good conscience, recommend two based on our experience. These are listed below. Also, remember that even though prices are far lower for both of these products in Pakistan, if the deal seems too good to be true then it probably is.

Bunyaad Carpets

rugs.tenthousandvillages.com
Bunyaad are a Lahore-based social enterprise that export almost all their carpets. They are a fair trade company that uses all organic products, and provides all those in the carpet chain with a fair living wage to keep local rug making a viable profession in Pakistan. They have produced a number of videos which will be helpful to anyone who wants to learn more about how a carpet is made, before going to buy one. *rugs.tenthousandvillages.com/rugs-101/ introduction-to-oriental-rugs-video/*. You can buy Bunyaad rugs in Pakistan, but you need to contact them to set up an appointment first by messaging them on Facebook: *facebook. com/bunyaad.rugs*.

Jewellery

There is no regulatory body for gems in Pakistan, so finding and using a reputable jeweller is critical. While there are many places to buy gemstones and jewellery in Lahore, we can only personally recommend two.

Stones & Beads Manufacturing Company

stones.beads@gmail.com
+92 423 652 3802
Stones and Beads Manufacturing Company has an amazing selection of gemstones, semi-precious stones and beads from Pakistan and Afghanistan. As they focus primarily on cutting and exporting stones they don't have much ready-made jewellery, but you can get exceptional deals on gemstones and then take them to a jeweller to have them set. Contact them for an appointment.

Karat

+92 423 587 4455
One reputable jeweller in Lahore is Karat. Located in Gulberg on Main Blvd, on the ground floor of the Empire Centre. (The building has a giant, lighted neon sign on top which reads 'Rafi Group'). It's best to go with an idea of what you want, or what you want made. They can set stones you have bought elsewhere. All gold used is 18 karat or higher.

SPECIALTY STORES

If you're looking for a gift or something special to take to a dinner there are a few stores where you can find specialty items.

Clayworks

clayworks.com
A boutique that makes clay pottery including all the fabulous 'I (heart) Pakistani city' mugs. They have two locations —a small shop in the Avari Hotel, and another in a residential building in Gulberg that's a bit hard to find, so don't be deterred. Call for directions and hours open.

Butler's Chocolate Café

facebook.com/butlerspk
Mmmm, yes, you read right, the 'purveyors of happiness', specialty chocolate shop from Ireland has a shop in Lahore...and right on M.M. Alam Road. A great alternative to bringing flowers to dinner at someone's house!

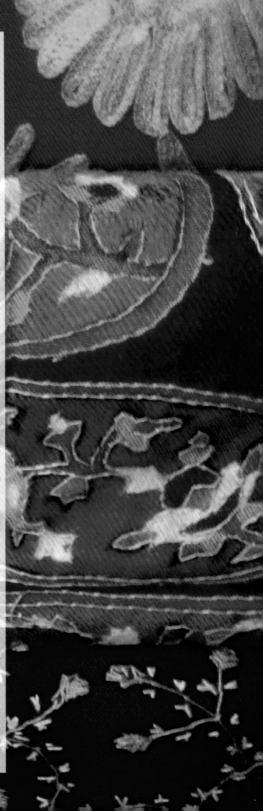

Bateel
bateel.com
The Saudi-based confectionary has a location in the Mall of Lahore where its date and dried fruit based confections can be found. Mmmm...chocolate dates. If you're invited to an iftar you won't go amiss turning up with these.

Flowers
If you need a last minute host(ess) present, flowers are always welcome. Large arrangements wrapped in ribbon, plastic and foil are the norm and can be found at any number of local flower markets through the city. A large arrangement will cost about the equivalent of $10-$20 USD. There is one flower market directly across from Liberty Market as well as one across from Data Darbar. Flowers in these open markets will be substantially cheaper than those bought in florist shops which are often foreign flowers. A dozen 'desi' roses should cost no more than $3 while they can be $2-5 a stem for imported roses.

Cigars & Tobacco
There used to be a widespread culture of hookah smoking at restaurants and cafes in Lahore, but this is now illegal. Hookahs are still available for sale for private use in some markets. Cigarettes are widely available at most stores, but for cigars and other specialty tobacco try:

- Cigar Lounge (in Nirvana Spa): Phone: +92 512 206 306; DHA
- Tobacco Masters: Phone: +92 423 589 0718; DHA Y Block, Shop No. 212
- Mr. Tobacco: Phone: +92 423 357 47135; DHA, 82-CCA Block DD, Phase 4

ARTS & CULTURE

Learn about Lahori literature, art and music

ARTS & CULTURE

Lahore is, indisputably, the cultural capital of Pakistan. Islamabad might be the capital and seat of politics and Karachi might be the beating heart of business, but without Lahore Pakistan would have no soul. Some of Pakistan's greatest writers, artists, and poets lived and died here infusing their works with a little of the city they loved. With the National College of Arts here and a long tradition of artists and writers 'in residence' there are plenty of opportunities to celebrate the arts and culture of Pakistan.

Museums & Cultural Centres

Alhamra Arts Centre
http://www.alhamra.gop.pk/
Located next to the Avari hotel on Mall Road the Alhamra Art Centre is a red brick building built in a modern style. Its architecture is meant to convey the essence of Mughal architecture found elsewhere in the city. The architect, Nayyar Ali Dada, won the Aga Khan award for architecture in 1998. This award is given to designers, architects or teams who build, or renovate, in Islamic societies. The complex was completed in 1992 and has a large auditorium, rooms for exhibitions, and art galleries.

Visiting: The Alhamra Centre is open during business hours but there is not much to see unless an exhibit or function being held there. Check their website for upcoming events.

Fakir Khana Museum
A little-known museum just inside Bhati gate in the Old City, the Fakir Khana is a private museum that houses the remarkable and eclectic collection of the Fakir family, descended from Muslim courtiers at the court of Sikh ruler Ranjit Singh. It is said to be the largest private collection in South Asia, with over 13,000 pieces of art including exquisite miniature paintings from the Sikh and Mughal period. There are also some fine examples of calligraphy from roughly the 18th or 19th century.

Visiting: As a private museum the Fakir Khana Museum is arranged only by private appointment by calling: +92 3354072145; +92 3009440684; or emailing: fakirkhanalahore@gmail.com.

The Lahore Museum

Designed by Bhai Ram Singh and built by Ganga Ram the Lahore Museum occupies a prominent place on Mall road. It opened in 1894 under the supervision of Lockwood Kipling – father of Rudyard Kipling - who was the principal of the School of Arts next door. While the displays are not always up to date it is worth a visit to see the beautiful building, the Gandhara (an ancient Greco-Buddhist civilisation centred around Peshawar during the 1st-5th centuries) collection, as well as ancient Pakistani pottery, jewellery, and manuscripts. Of particular note is the 'Fasting Buddha', which is world renowned.

Visiting: Entrance to the museum is on the left side of the museum if viewing from the street. Tickets for foreigners cost 400 rupees and are bought at a small window to the right of the museum entrance.

Allama Iqbal Museum (Javed Manzil)

Muhammad (Allama) Iqbal is Pakistan's most prominent poet and philosopher. He is credited with inspiring the Pakistan movement, and was knighted by King George V. His house, named Javed Manzil after his son Javed, was converted into a museum in 1961 and declared a national monument in 1977. Today it preserves and displays his personal effects, memorabilia and manuscripts.

Visiting: The Museum is located on Allama Iqbal Road not far from the Railway Station and the Old City. It is normally open during working hours but is currently closed for renovation.

Dabistan-e-Iqbbal

Dabistan-e-Iqbal is an institution set up by Iqbal's family to spread the vision and ideas of Allama Iqbal including Iqbal's view of a modern Muslim state. They have collected a treasury of Iqbal'ss work and regularly hold lectures, debates, and post otherwise unseen photos and videos of

Visiting: The Dabistan-e-Iqbal is located in Gulberg across from the Home Economics College. It open to the public and visitors can make an appointment by phoning: +92 (0) 42 357 786 88 or emailing info@dabistaneiqbal.com. Visit: *web.facebook.com/DabistaneIqbal/?_rdr*

The Shakir Ali Museum

web.facebook.com/Shakir-ali-museum-Institution-Educational-Cultural-Govt-120864328002611/?_rdr
Shakir Ali (1916-1975) was an influential modern Pakistani painter and artist. He was the first Head of the Art Department at the National College of Arts after it opened and became the principal from 1971-1973. Many of his works are collected in a museum formed in his house, which is also a beautiful piece of Lahori architecture. The museum also exhibits other contemporary artists and holds workshops

Visiting: Between Gulberg and Model Town, the museum is at 93, Shakir Ali Lane, Tipu Block, New Garden Town. Call or email before visiting to ensure it is open and +92 (0) 311 565 4552 / shakiramuseum@gmail.com.

Peeru's Puppetry Museum

facebook.com/Peerus.Cafe

Peeru's Café is better known for its food and live performances of Sufi and Ghazal music than it's puppet museum, which is tucked behind the open courtyard. However, the museum is well done and collects anitque and contemporary fold puppets. It is worth a wander as it collects and preserves a piece of folk history which is little known. At times they will hold puppet shows and you should call to find out when.

Visiting: Located out Raiwind road about 30 minutes from Gulberg the museum is usually open when Peeru's is so go have dinner, take in the music and see the puppets!

Naqsh School of Arts & Gallery

naqsh.org/naqsh-gallery.html

The small Naqsh art gallery deserves special mention as it is part of the Naqsh School of Arts a school which provides low-cost arts education to underprivileged youth in the Old City. Set in the courtyard of a beautiful old haveli, students learn both traditional and modern art skills such as calligraphy, miniature painting, ceramics and graphic design. Their gallery is an excellent place to buy a piece of original artwork at affordable prices while supporting the school. If you'll be in Lahore a bit longer you should go to their annual exhibition of art by the graduating class. You an also ask for a schedule of the classes offered and sign up to learn these arts yourself!

Visiting: Naqsh is open from 9-5 Monday through Saturday and some hours on Sunday if you want to visit the gallery & shop. A MUST see on your tour of the Old City! Contact them by calling or through their Facebook page.

Truck Art

All around Lahore you will see trucks (and sometimes buses, vans, rickshaws and animal carts) colourfully painted top to bottom with bright colours and adorned with jingling metal and mirrors. Welcome to the world of South Asian Truck Art. The exact origin of decorating trucks (also called 'Jingle Trucks') in Pakistan is unknown but it is thought to have begun as a way to attract customers and increase revenue. It is also likely associated with good luck and warding off evil spirits. Along with the truck's exterior, the cabins of the trucks are decorated as this is believed to help keep drivers awake on monotonous journeys. To paint a complete truck can cost between $3,000-$5,000 USD. Most of the writing on trucks is either advertisement for the company, or person, who owns it or pithy sayings in Urdu, Pashto or Punjabi.

Truck art has now taken on a life of its own - no longer confined only to vehicle. Truck artists will paint just about anything and truck art has begun appearing on tables, chairs, signs, and even in contemporary art.

Jamal Elias has studied truck art and written a beautiful book called *On Wings of Diesel*.

"Lahore was often called the 'The Paris of the East.' [sic]...The similarity lay not in the city's outward appearance or its historic role but in the joyous and carefree atmosphere that marked Lahore's cultural life, with its numerous cafes and restaurants, noisy receptions and festivals, and elegantly dressed crowds strolling on the Mall."

– Anna Suvorova

Art & Art Galleries

Art might be Lahore's best kept secret. Without public places to display and a lack of public attention to art in the country, Pakistani artists are definitely more the talk of the art world internationally than at home. While they're out winning global art awards and being shown in other capitals they receive relatively little attention here. This means that whether you're a collector or you're just looking for a piece to remember your time in Pakistan buying art in Lahore is a very good idea. It's possible to buy pieces in Pakistan that would go for thousands more in a gallery in New York or Delhi. Pakistan artists are talented, relevant, and their pieces are worth the investment. And, while Karachi is the town with the real art scene, and most of the galleries, Lahore is the town with all the artists. If you're looking for a specific

piece of contemporary, or modern, art you might have to search a bit but you can definitely find it in Lahore.

The best way to get in contact with most galleries is to either contact them through Facebook or to call. Many have a mailing list which will send emails prior to events and shows. A number of the galleries also have talks and special exhibitions so make sure to check their Facebook page frequently.

Art galleries in Lahore span a spectrum from glorified framing shops which sell replicas of Pakistani masters to permanent exhibition spaces which are like mini-museums. It is important to know what type of piece you are looking for before you begin. If you're a collector or want a piece as an investment (in the $200-thousands USD range) then only visit the contemporary galleries listed below. These galleries are almost exclusively by appointment only unless you are invited to an exhibition shown there. If you're looking for something more affordable that is likely to have captured a Pakistani landscape, cultural site, or portrait try one of the modern art galleries listed below. For any serious investment do ask the gallery for the artist's certificate to prove it is genuine.

Contemporary Art Galleries

Continuing its long tradition as a centre for art and culture, Lahore today boasts a thriving contemporary art scene that is gaining increasing recognition globally. Political turmoil, violence, increasing fundamentalism and a general shrinking of civic space have provided a stimulus for creativity that has led to a contemporary renaissance in the arts. Fine art institutions such as the hallowed National College of Arts and the newer Beaconhouse National University provide safe spaces in which artists can express their sensibilities. These art colleges offer rigorous technical training, notably in the traditional Mughal art of miniature painting at the NCA, which has been subverted and made new by world-renowned artists such as Shahzia Sikander, Imran Qureshi and Ayesha Khalid. These artists' works, costing tens of thousands of dollars, are not usually available locally. But there are plenty of younger artists, taught by established and practicing artists at Lahore's art institutions, whose work can be seen and purchased. Some of the leading galleries in Lahore are listed below. Check in advance if they are open and have an exhibition on. Also, if you're serious about collecting make sure to attend NCA's annual thesis display of their graduating class where you can buy artwork before artists have made names for themselves.

Alhamra - Lahore Arts Council

The permanent gallery at the Alhamra— Lahore Arts Council has a small collection of works by modern and contemporary Pakistani artists. They periodically have solo exhibitions of emerging and established artists.
Phone: +92 42 99230791

Gallery 39K

A gallery showcasing emerging contemporary artists, both from Pakistan and abroad. They aim to be innovative and engaging in the shows they curate.
facebook.com/gallery39k
Phone: +92 301 843 4093
Address: 39-K, Model Town, gallery39k@gmail.com

Rohtas 2

This is the offshoot of the original Rohtas Gallery in Islamabad that launched the career of many a young artist. It is run by Salima Hashmi, artist and writer of many definitive books on Pakistani contemporary art. She is currently the Dean of Visual Arts at Beaconhouse University. Asad Hayee is a curator here.

The gallery is not well advertised, but the combined expertise of Salima and Asad make it well worth visiting if you can get hold of them.
Phone: +92 423 588 4044
Address: 156-G Model Town, Lahore, Pakistan
info@rohtasgallery.com / rohtasgallery@gmail.com

Taseer Art Gallery

Originally called the Drawing Room and run by her father, Sanam Taseer shows both emerging and established contemporary artists. Almost all of the artists there are to know will pass through Taseer Gallery. Call ahead to arrange a viewing.
www.taseerartgallery.com/
facebook.com/Taseerartgallery
Phone: +92 300 844 3273
taseerartgallery@gmail.com

Zahoor Ul Akhlaq Gallery

Established in 1993 and named after one of the pioneers of contemporary art in Pakistan, tragically murdered in 1999. It is located within the National College of Art. Apart from a small permanent collection, the gallery mounts exhibitions that are used to teach students critical and curatorial practice.
facebook.com/Zahoor-ul-Akhlaq-Gallery
Phone: +92 (0) 42 9210 599 / 9210 601
Address: National College of Arts, No. 4 Shahrah-e-Quaid-e-Azam

Modern Art Galleries

Nairang Gallery
nairanggalleries.com
facebook.com/nairang.art
Phone: +92 42 37421202
Email: nairangart@gmail.com
Address: 101-Habitat Flats, Jail

Ejaz Art Gallery
ejazartgallery.com/
facebook.com/ejazartgalleries
Phone: +92 42 35762784 / +92 42 35762784
Address: 79 B/1 MM Alam Road,

The Collectors Galleria
collectorsgalleria.com
facebook.com/thecollectorsgalleria
Phone : +92 42 35751512
Address: Alhamra Cultural Complex, Gaddafi
Stadium, Ferozepur Road

Coopera Art Gallery
facebook.com/CooperaArtGallery
Phone: +92 42 37321161
Address: 70, Shahrah-e-Quaid-e-Azam
Lahore

Hamail Art Gallery
hamailartgalleries.com
facebook.com/hamailartgalleries
Phone: +92 42 35771204-7
Address: 67 C-1, Off M, M, Alam Road,
opposite KFC Gulberg III

Native Art Gallery
nativeartgallery.com.pk
Phone: +92-042-35732346
Address: 161/5, Sector H, DHA 1

Revivers Galleria
reviversgalleria.com
facebook.com/Revivers-Galleria
Phone: +92-42-35872760; +92-42-35872761
Address: ISA Tower,84-B-1, Ghalib Road,
Gulberg III

Unicorn Gallery
unicorngalleryblog.com
facebook.com/unicorngallery
Phone: +92 (0) 42 35777660; +92 (0) 300
8260580
Address: 32-B-2, Main Gulberg, Lahore

Literature

A Lahore Reading List

A trip to Lahore would not be complete without dipping into some of the rich writing there is about the city both by Pakistani and foreign authors. Seeing the city through the eyes of writers can help you gain insight into the city as it is now and as it used to be. Below is a reading list and almost all titles you can find either on Amazon, in the Lahore bookstores listed on page ? or you can visit either Sang-e-Meel Publications (*sangemeel.com*) located at the end of Mall Road or Ferozsons (*ferozsons.com.pk*) also on Mall Road.

Fiction:

◆ *The Crow Eaters* - by Bapsi Sidhwa
◆ *Cracking India* (originally *The Ice Candy Man*) - by Bapsi Sidhwa
◆ *Moth Smoke* – by Mohsin Hamid
◆ *The Reluctant Fundamentalist* - by Mohsin Hamid
◆ *Queens Road* – by Sorayya Khan

Non-Fiction:

◆ *The Illustrated Beloved City, Writings on Lahore* - edited by Bapsi Sidhwa
◆ *City of Sin and Splendour: Writings on Lahore* - edited by Bapsi Sidhwa
◆ *The Dancing Girls of Lahore* – by Louise Brown
◆ *Lahore: A Sentimental Journey* - by Pran Nevile
◆ *Illustrated Views of the 19th Century* - by F.S. Aijazuddin
◆ *Lahore: Portrait of a Lost City* - by Som Anand
◆ *Lahore: A Memoir* - by Muhammad Saeed
◆ *101 Tales of a Fabled City* - by Majid Sheikh
◆ *Lahore: Tales Without End* - by Majid Sheikh
◆ *Lahore: The City Within* - by Samina Quraeshi
◆ *Discontent and its Civilizations: Dispatches from Lahore, New York, and London* – Mohsin Hamid
◆ *Making Lahore Modern: Constructing and Imagining a Colonial City*
◆ – by William Glover
◆ *The Bargain from the Bazaar: A Family's Day of Reckoning in Lahore* – by Haroon Ullah
◆ *Lahore: Its History, Architectural Remains, and Antiquities* – by Syad Muhammad Latif
◆ *Lahore Recollected* – by F.S. Aijazuddin
◆ *The Coffee House of Lahore: A Memoir (1942-1957)* - by K.K. Aziz
◆ *The Walled City of Lahore – Sustainable Development of the Walled City of Lahore Project – 2009*

Lahori Writers

Several other, notable writers are especially known for their residence in Lahore.

Allama Muhammad Iqbal (1877-1938): Iqbal is Pakistan's national poet and philosopher and cited as being the inspiration of the Pakistan movement which called for the creation of Pakistan. His birthday is a national holiday celebrated on November 9th each year. He died in Lahore and is buried just outside the Badshahi mosque in the Old City. He wrote extensively in both Urdu and Persian and had approximately 12,000 poems by the time of his death. He was knighted in 1922 by the English King George V.

Saadat Hasan Manto (1912-1955): Manto is considered one of the greatest Pakistani writers producing a huge volume of work during his life – including short stories, essays, a play and a novel. He was originally from Bombay but moved to Lahore during Partition,

Lahore The

LAHORE

LAHORE

HEIKH ✦ Lahore

LAHORE

WRITINGS ON LAHORE

LAHORE RECOLLECTIO

which he writes about in his work. After moving to Lahore he became associated with the Pak Tea House where other writers and intellectuals of his day gathered. He was tried for obscenity six times but never convicted. Fifty years after his death he was commemorated on a Pakistan stamp and he was also awarded the Nishan-e-Imtiaz by the government in 2012.

Intizar Hussain (1923-2016): Hussain is possibly the best known Pakistani writer after Manto. He was born in India and his family moved to Lahore during Partition. He wrote a number of novels, poetry, and short stories as well as writing for daily newspapers in Lahore. He was shortlisted for the Man Booker Prize in 2013 for his work, *Basti*.

Faiz Ahmed Faiz (1911–1984): was one of Pakistan's most prominent poets. A member of the Progressive Writers Movement, he was awarded, in 1962, the Lenin Prize by the Soviet Union. Nominated for the Nobel Prize in literature four times and the Nobel Peace Prize once he has, posthumously, been awarded Pakistan's highest civil award—the Nishan-e-Imtiaz.

Literature Festivals , Events & Foundations

Faiz Foundation Trust
faizghar.net/calendar.php
Faiz's family has set up a foundation to honour his ideas of 'struggle for social justice through the arts'. The Foundation routinely holds concerts, readings, and classes which are open to the public. In 2015, they also held the Faiz International Festival with authors and artists coming together to honour his life's work.

Lahore Literary Festival
www.lahorelitfest.com/
The LLF is known by its iconic logo and for bringing together each year some of the most interesting writers, politicians, artists and thinkers from Pakistan and abroad for a week of events. Finding out the dates can be a bit tricky as they don't advertise them much in advance but it normally takes place during the third weekend of February at the Alhamra Arts Centre. If you have to pick a single event to attend in Lahore each year this is it. Entry is free.

Alhamra International Literary & Cultural Festival

www.alhamra.gop.pk

The Lahore Arts Council holds an annual literary festival which was expanded in 2015 to include dance, music, and art exhibitions. It usually takes place at the end of the year – November or December in the Alhamra Arts Centre. Entry is free.

The Last Word

facebook.com/TheLastWordbks

If you're looking for book readings, poetry slam, or talks on fascinating topics make sure to look at The Last Word Bookshop's Facebook page to see what they have on.

The Pak Tea House

The Pak Tea House's name is synonymous with arts, literature, and culture in Lahore. Most popular in the 1950's-60's, it was frequented by some of the great names in art including poet Faiz Ahmed Faiz, writer Saadat Hasan Manto, and singer Ustad Amanat Ali Khan. The tea house also became synonymous with the socialist Progressive Writers' Movement which began in India in the 1930's and called for social justice and development. The Pak Tea House was shut down in the early 2000's but was reopened by the government of Punjab in 2013. It still sits near the junction of Mall road and Jamal-ud-Din road in the Anarkali neighbourhood. There is a blog now by the same name (*pakteahouse.net*) which aims to "revive the culture of debate, pluralism and tolerance".

"The Pak Tea House was not merely a place where writers hung out and passionately discussed literature, the arts, and politics, or where they held their literary meetings and dreamed their brave, fragile dreams, or where they stopped on their way to and from work every day for a brief chat, it was unique as a gathering place which never denied its hospitality to anyone, even those who could not afford to pay for a cup of tea. It chose to operate at a loss rather than submit to the indignity of closing its doors to the nation's destitute and chronically disenfranchised intellectuals. It was everything the society at large was not – and above all it was a place where dreams could be dreamed, where time and history could be held at bay."

—Muhammad Umar Memon

Music

In Lahore, there are few large public concerts but you can still find all types of music if you know where to look. Keep an eye out in the local English language papers, but also make sure to visit some of the different websites below. In the meantime, you can get a taste of some of the music of Lahore by visiting the music links listed here. Music in Lahore tends to reflect a few different musical traditions:

Punjabi Folk Music

Like most folk music, Punjabi folk focuses on the different seasons of life and major events including love, longing, marriage, bravery, conflict and death. Both traditional and modern Punjabi folk music can be heard at: *folkpunjab.org*. Arif Lohar is one popular and lively Punjabi folk musician. Watch him perform one of his most famous songs, Jungi Ji, here: *youtube.com/watch?v=IzHe4K_3j08*.

Qawwali

Qawwali is a form of Sufi devotional music that is a fusion of Persian, Indian, Arabic and Turkish traditional styles. The lyrics are drawn from Persian, Urdu and Punjabi poetry as well as regional dialects such as Saraiki, but in Pakistan qawwali is mostly sung in Urdu and Punjabi. It is performed by a group of eight to ten men, comprising one or two lead singers, one or two playing the tabla (percussion), a harmonium player, and a supporting chorus who repeat the lines of the lead singers and provide hand clapping. Most songs are at least 15 minutes long and some as long as an hour. Most songs are in worship of Allah, the Prophet Muhammad (PBUH), or Sufi saints, and aim to produce in the listener a state of spiritual ecstasy. Sufi.com has compiled

a list of their top 100 qawwalis and you can have a listen here: *thesufi.com/sufimusic/100-best-qawwali-music-tracks-ever.html*. Nusrat Fateh Ali Khan (1948-1977) is a particularly popular, and perhaps most well-known, qawwali singer and his family has followed in his footsteps with his nephew Rahat Fateh Ali Khan also being a popular singer. Other singers to listen for are: Ghulam Farid Sabri, Amjad Sabri, who was tragically murdered in 2016, and Santoo Khan.

Ghazals

Closely linked with the Sufi tradition, Ghazals are a form of poetry sung in a traditional, light-classical style. Ghazals themes are normally about love, beauty, pain, and loss. Nearly every Lahori will know a large number of ghazals by heart and popular ghazal singers include: Barkhat Ali Khan (*youtube.com/watch?v=GDUqbsitVaw*), Mehdi Hasan (*youtube.com/watch?v=qcKxMW6aLnk*), and Ghulam Ali (*youtube.com/watch?v=j3_CkTWf5HE*).

Bhangra

Popularised in the 1980's there is

some debate about whether bhangra is a new or old Punjabi musical tradition. It was certainly reinvented by the Pakistani and Indian diaspora by blending Punjabi folk music with more popular pop sounds, and has even taken the form of exercise classes in Europe and North America. If you want to see Bhangra performed, Bhangra Empire has a number of recorded performances on Youtube: *youtube.com/user/BhangraEmpire*.

Pakistani Pop/Rock

There are a number of extremely popular Pakistani pop and rock groups which have their roots in Lahore. Junoon, for example, (*youtube.com/watch?v=MU_hK092m5o*) and Bilal Khan (*bilalkhanmusic.com/music*) are two worth watching. Junoon is reportedly launching a new album in celebration of their 25th anniversary.

Live Music, Festivals & Foundations

Peeru's Café

facebook.com/Peerus.Cafe
Your best bet for seeing live music on a regular basis in Lahore is Peerus. While they have music several weeknights they usually always have Sufi music on Thursdays. Played in an open courtyard while dinner is served this is a must. Check the Facebook page which is regularly updated with upcoming events.

All Pakistan Music Conference (APMC)

facebook.com/APMCPakistan
Founded in 1959 as a way to keep the traditional and classical music traditions of Pakistan alive the APMC holds both monthly music concerts as well as a large annual conference.

Lahore Music Meet

http://lahoremusicmeet.com/
https://web.facebook.com/lahoremusicmeet/
An annual, two-day event held at the Alhamra Cultural Centre, Lahore Music Meet brings together musicians and fans to hear performances, panels discussions and lectures about music in Pakistan. It is usually held in the spring (March/April) and their Facebook page can also keep you updated on musical happenings in Lahore and elsewhere in Pakistan.

Coke Studio

cokestudio.com.pk/season9
Now in its 9th season, Coke Studio is a television series which features popular and well-known Pakistani artists recording music in their different styles. Many of the videos can be watched online and it's a great way to see the different styles and artists of Pakistan.

Shrine of Baba Shah Jamal

Sufi saint Shah Jamal died in Lahore in 1671. His tomb has become a shrine near Model Town, not far from Gulberg off Canal Bank Road. Every Thursday, devotees gather to listen to drummers and enter a trance-like devotional state, dancing like whirling dervishes. Papu Sain, a famous sufi dhol (drum) player, often plays on Thursdays. Both incense and hashish use is common, and foreigners should take care when visiting.

Rafi Peer Theatre

rafipeer.com
acebook.com/Rafipeertheatreworkshop
Based in Lahore, the Rafi Peer Theater intermittently holds theatre and music events. They also host the Annual International Mystic Music Sufi Festival featuring national and international Sufi singers.

Song of Lahore - the Movie

facebook.com/SongofLahore
www.songoflahoremovie.com

A brilliant new film which has been nominated for a number of independent film awards follows the story of the traditional musicians of Sachal Studios in Lahore as they fuse traditional Pakistani music with jazz catching global attention. This includes the attention of American jazz great, Wynton Marsalis, who invites them to perform with him and the Lincoln Center Orchestra in New York. The movie is a story of their journey as well as their mission to revive traditional music in Pakistan.

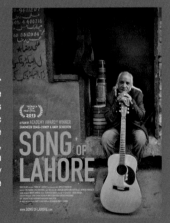

Finding out what's happening...

"When you are born in Lahore you are connected to a collective consciousness," a friend explained when asked how Lahoris just seem to know what is happening, when, and where. While having access to that consciousness is great if you're from Lahore it can be especially aggravating if you are just visiting. Information about arts and culture events is spread by word of mouth and sometimes doesn't show up in papers or on social media feeds until after the fact. You can spend your time attempting to mine information from your Lahori friends or obsessively websites and facebook pages. Obviously, this isn't ideal if you, say, have a job. Websites tend to advertise events only a day or two before they occur – if at all. So, until the 'collective consciousness' is made public there are a couple of websites which list events and if you check the below you can sometimes keep up with upcoming events.

- ◆ Youlin Magazine is a cultural journal covering Pakistan and China. Their Lahore page is one of the most up-to-date places to find cultural events in Lahore. *youlinmagazine.com/upcoming-events-in-lahore*
- ◆ ArtNow Pakistan: *artnowpakistan.com*
- ◆ All eventsLahore: *allevents.in/lahore*
- ◆ Happening PK: *happening.pk/lahore*
- ◆ *Danka: danka.pk*
- ◆ My Art World: *facebook.com/myartworldgallery*

ACTIVITIES

Get out and play

Recreation & Exercise

PARKS

If you're looking to get out and moving, a trip to any number of parks in Lahore will do the trick. Most of them have nice walking tracks just inside the perimeter that are used during the day by numbers of Lahoris. A google map search will show you one in your area and you can zoom

in to see the walking track. It is advisable to walk and run during daylight hours only. Running on the road is not advisable due to road and driving conditions in Pakistan. There are lots of cyclists in Lahore, but they are usually labourers or children bicycling for transportation rather than pleasure or exercise. Extreme caution should be used when attempting to cycle in Lahore and it isn't generally advisable.

Jilani Park (Racecourse Park/Polo Club Park)

Jilani is a park in Gulberg with a large track (approximately 2.7 km) just within the perimeter. Lahore Polo Club is found in the middle of the park which also contains cricket grounds, a small lake, playgrounds, and an amusement park.

Model Town Park

A circular park right in the middle of Model Town, there is a track (approximately 2.3 km) that circles the perimeter. There is also a playground and boating area.

Lawrence Gardens (Jinnah Gardens, The Botanical Gardens)

Lawrence Gardens on Mall Road is famous for its historic botanical gardens and is popular with families and people out for a walk. The walking track (approximately 1.9 km) weaves around the park with plenty of different paths to meander down. There are also tennis courts, but you have to be a member of the Punjab tennis association to use them.

Jallo Park

If you take Canal Bank Road past the Ring Road Junction, approximately half an hour from the city centre you'll reach Jallo Park. Along with Changa Manga and the Lahore Zoo it is a wildlife park funded by the Punjab Wildlife and Parks Department. There is a large pond for boating and a track for walking and cycling as well as lawn tennis courts.

GOLF

Lahore boasts five golf courses and you don't need to be a member of the clubs to play. Bear in mind that during the summer months it can be difficult to get a tee time as the only hours where it's possible contemplate being outside are at five and six am – and even then it's blazing hot! Each course will also have their own dress code so make sure to be informed of that before you turn up. The Royal Palm requires you to take a test in order to play.

Defence Golf Course
www.drgcc.com
facebook.com/DefenceRaya
Home of the Punjab Open Golf Tournament, the Defence course is in Phase 3 of DHA. It has 18 holes and you can take a walk-through of each hole on their website.

Lahore Garrison Course
www.lggcc.com.pk
In the heart of Cantt, not far from the airport is the Lahore Garrison Golf Course. It is a 72-par course with 18 holes.

Oasis Course
www.theoasis.com.pk
Approximately an hour's drive from Lahore you'll find the Oasis Golf Course. It's a 9 hole, 36-par course and also has a driving range.

Lahore Gymkhana Course
www.lahoregymkhana.com.pk/facilities/golf/
Founded in the late 1800's the Gymkhana course is one of the oldest golf courses in Pakistan. In the heart of Lahore, it is home to the Punjab Amateur and Governor's Cup and is 72-par with 18 holes and also has a floodlit driving range.

Royal Palm Course
www.rpgcc.com
Also right in central Lahore just off Canal Bank Road is the Royal Palm golf course. It is 72-par with 18 holes and a two-tier, floodlit driving range. A description of each hole can be found on their website.

TENNIS, POOLS, HEALTH & FITNESS CENTRES

Pools and gyms in Lahore are limited but there are still a number of good options for visitors. If you're in town for only a short while and are looking for a pool or gym find out if your hotel has one before booking—many do. These hotels will sometimes allow non-guests to access for a fee. If you're staying longer, or at a hotel without these, simply call, or visit, the fitness centre and find out if you can buy a month, or week, membership. Their marketing departments are usually quite happy to help. Before you pay, or sign up for a membership, do take a tour of the facilities and ask for all the details that interest you. Simply because it's on the website doesn't mean it's available. Many memberships require a one-off, sign-up fee, a monthly fee, and then a pay-per-use for things like the squash court or yoga classes. Try to find this out up front. Also, some locations have segregated gyms, pools or hours, for men and women. You will want to know if this is the case and whether those timings work for you.

Structures (Gym, pool)
structure.com.pk
Structures is a 'fitness boutique' in the Residency Hotel in Gulburg and in DHA. It has an 18m pool outdoor pool with both adult and child swimming lessons available. Additionally, they have an executive mixed gym, jacuzi, sauna, and studio classes like crossfit, boot camp, Zumba, and pilates/yoga. Personal training is available. There is a bar serving smoothies, juices, sandwiches, detox juices, and energy drinks in the lobby. If you're staying at the Residency you can use the facilities for 1,000 a day.

Sukh Chan Wellness Club (Gym, pool, spa, squash)
www.sukh-chan.com
Located in Gulberg, the Sukh Chan Wellness Club is near the well-known Salt'n'Pepper Grill and has a large number of services available to members. Open 7am to 10pm they have a swimming pool, spa, steam room and sauna, salon, squash courts, fitness classes (yoga, pilates, Zumba, step, etc.). Short term visitors should contact them, or drop by, for more information about using the facilities.

Pearl Continental (Gym, pool)
www.pchotels.com/pclahore/en/facilities
The Pearl Continental has a gym and spa offering a wide range of packages. The outdoor, 25m pool is available for non-guest use for a fee. Contact the hotel for more information.

Gold Spa & Fitness Club (Gym, pool, spa)
goldspaandfitness.com
Gold Spa and Fitness Club has a wide range of spa treatments as well as a gym with machines and free weights and lap pool. It is located in the Mall of Lahore which is in

Cantt which foreigners might have trouble accessing. Short term visitors should contact them, or drop by, for more information about using the facilities.

Shapes (Gym, spa)
facebook.com/ShapesActive
Shapes has three locations: Gulberg, DHA and Model Town. Each of these have gym, fitness classes, and personal trainers available. Memberships vary so contact the location near you for more details.

The Nishat (Gym, pool)
nishathotels.com/pages/wellness/gym-45/
Centrally located in the Nishat Hotel in Gulberg the Nishat offers its gym and indoor pool for use by members as well as guests. Contact the hotel to find out more about short-term memberships or one time use.

Avari Hotel (Gym, pool)
www.avari.com/property/avari-lahore/wellness-leisure
The Avari hotel has a 25m pool and also allows non-guests to use the pool and gym for a fee. Contact the hotel for more information

Royal Palm Golf & Country Club (Gym, pool, spa, squash, tennis)
www.rpgcc.com
Tennis courts, squash courts, two swimming pools, personal trainers and fitness classes are all available at the Royal Palm, a membership only club right off Canal Bank Road. Contact the club for more information about short-term use.

Gymkhana (Gym, pool, spa, squash, tennis)
www.lahoregymkhana.com.pk/sauna-wellness-center
The Lahore Gymkhana, in all its aging glory, really does have it all—three pools, squash courts, several gyms, classes, golf, as well as access to all the other amenities. However, there is a hefty, annual, $3,000 USD sign-up fee for foreigners plus the monthly membership fee as well as fees for use of each facility (e.g. pool use, gym use, golf, etc.) There is no daily, weekly, monthly membership.

SQUASH

It's a little known fact that Pakistan once dominated the squash world and continues to have a love for the sport producing many fine squash players. From the 1950's to 1990's, Pakistani players brought home over 30 British Open titles and 14 World Open titles. If you're looking for a good game of squash you're sure to find it at any number of squash courts in Lahore. Many of these will have 'squash ladders' where you can sign up to meet and play new people.

- ◆ Punjab Squash Association – facebook.com/PunjabSquashComplex
- ◆ Civil Officers Mess at Punjab Civil Officers Mess Lahore
- ◆ Gymkhana
- ◆ Defence Club
- ◆ Royal Palm

POLO

The polo scene in Lahore is very active and it is home to the Lahore Polo Club—one of the oldest in South Asia. Polo was likely invented in Persia as early as the 6th century BC and spread throughout South Asia long before it was 'discovered' by the British when they occupied India. One of the oldest tombs in Lahore is that of Qutb-ud-Din Aibak, a slave-king who rose from slavery to rule in 1206 and famously died playing the precursor to polo in 1210. The polo grounds in Race Course Park are named for him.

There are two polo grounds in Lahore with international standard fields and play. Polo is a winter sport in Pakistan so most of the games will be in the winter/spring. The first is the Aibak Ground in Jilani Park (Gulberg) and the second is in Cantt off the Lahore-Bedian road.

Most polo games are held in tournaments sponsored by various businesses and include international teams and players coming to Lahore. Tickets, or an invitation, are normally necessary and to find out when upcoming games are contact the Lahore Polo Club: *lahorepoloclub.com/contact_us.htm* To find out more about upcoming tournaments visit the websites listed.

- Lahore Polo Club: *lahorepoloclub. com; facebook.com/Lahore-Polo-Club-239291229459682*
- Pakistan Polo Association: *pakpolo.org/ polopakistan*
- Lahore Garrison Polo Club: *lgspc.net*

"Perhaps this is the word that best captures the city of Lahore: romance.... Romance floats in the very air of Lahore, between the molecules of pollution and the aroma of food cooking at every street corner....Lahoris also experience this romance when they recall the haunts of their childhood... They recall the feel of the grass of the Race Course Park when they ran barefoot across its lawn; the taste of the jamun and mangoes picked from trees planted at their grandparents' houses; or the heavy fragrance of motia.... Lahoris are indeed a very sentimental people."

–Bina Shah, *A Love Affair with Lahore*

CRICKET

It's not hard to find a cricket game in Lahore. Kids play in the streets, adults play on their work breaks—just about every park will have a game (or 50) of cricket going at any time. However, if it's professional cricket you're after then you'll have to go to Dubai. Sadly, in 2009, the Sri Lankan team was attacked by a terrorist group in Lahore and it all but ended international cricket in Pakistan. Since then there has only been one international tour (consisting of a three One Day International and two Twenty20 International matches) when Zimbabwe came to play in Gadaffi Stadium in May 2015.

Amateur cricket is played in a number of first-class cricket grounds in Lahore. The oldest, and most famous ground, is the Gymkhana (Bagh-e-Jinnah) ground in Jilani Park. Almost all the universities have a cricket ground as do several of the high schools. Model Town, DHA, and several other neighbourhoods have cricket grounds.

The Lahore Lions are the local cricket team and routinely play against 19 other domestic teams—usually in Gadaffi Stadium if they're playing at home. Upcoming games can be found here: *sportsdepth.com/team/lahore-lions-73/*

To follow the Pakistan team go to the Pakistan Cricket Board's website: *www.pcb.com.pk*

PAINTBALL / GO KARTING

facebook.com/Battlefield.Lahore
Not far from the airport in DHA is Battlefield Lahore. Here they have paintballing, go karts, zipline, and a bunjee trampoline.

MOVIE THEATRES

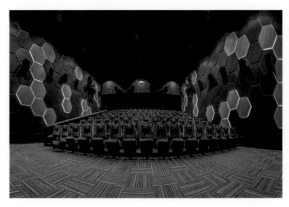

Lahore has thirteen movie theatres which show both Pakistani and international movies. If you're thinking of watching a Pakistani movie call ahead and find out if there are subtitles in English as not all movies theatres will have them. The most convenient movie theatres for visitors are listed below. If you want to see what is on at all the theatres in Lahore visit: *easytickets.pk* and search Lahore theatres.

Cine Star IMAX

cinestar.com.pk
This is the only IMAX theatre in Lahore and is located in Civic Centre Township just south of Model Town. It has only one screen in a large theatre that can seat 581 but tickets do sell out quickly. If you're going to see the latest action-packed blockbuster this is where to go. The theatre has plenty of snacks and a Burger King in the lobby.

DHA Cinema

dha3d4kcinema.com
This cinema is in R Block of DHA. It has only one screen and while there is plenty of space the screen is seems small and people tend to 'interact' with movies here more than elsewhere. Parking used to be limited but they have expanded behind the cinema.

Super Cinema

supercinema.com.pk
Located in the Vogue Towers on M.M. Alam Road this theatre has three screens but is often packed on the weekends and it can be

hard to get tickets. Parking is also difficult to non-existent.

Cinepax Fortress Mall

cinepax.com/cinemas
This theatre is in Cantt so visitors should make sure they leave time to enter. Located just over the Mian Mir Bridge inside the Fortress Mall. There is one screen and a medium-sized theatre.

Super Cinema

supercinema.com.pk
Found in Royal Palm and Country Club complex there are three theatres which hold around 100 people each. They show 3D movies here.

Cinegold

cinegold.com.pk
A bit out of the way in Bahria Town, CineGold tends to play Bollywood and Pakistani movies in a large, single-screen theatre.

SPAS & SALONS

Pakistanis of all genders frequent spas and salons and can spend a vast amount of a day there. Most spas and salons will have the standard menu of services, haircuts & dye, manicures & pedicures, massages, facials as well as an assortment of other treatments. By Western standards spas in Lahore are fairly inexpensive with a manicure/pedicure only costing about $20 USD. The major hotels will tend to offer spa and salon services but call to ensure if you're planning to use them as their staff are not always available. Opinions about spas vary. Some are cheap and cheerful and some aim to give a holistic spa experience.

Hifsa Khan Salon & Studio
facebook.com/hifsa.k.salon
Hifsa Khan's salon is right on the edge of Cantt just over Sher Pao bridge on Abid Majeed Road (near Shezan bakery). They offer a full range of services and specialise in sea-based products.

Nirvana Day Spa & Salon
nirvana.com.pk
It's hard to miss Nirvana's new spa and salon in Phase 5 of DHA as it occupies three stories and 55,000 square feet. It's truly a place you can spend a day with a café (and a cigar lounge) as well as a full range of day spa and salon services.

Arramish Spa
arammish.com
In a quiet residential area of Gulberg, tucked off Canal Bank Road is Arramish. It has a small café and offers a full range of services and therapies including Aruyveda.

Toni & Guy
toniandguy.com
The London-based salon has two locations in Lahore. One on M.M. Alam road and another in Phase 3, Z block of DHA. Primarily a hair salon they also have a limited number of other services.

ACTIVITIES FOR KIDS

Pakistan is a great country for kids. Pakistanis value family and welcome children at almost any location or event. Whether it's in a park, historic site or restaurant, you'll find children there. Be aware, if you are a foreigner, some Pakistanis will want to photograph foreign children and be in photographs with them. Most mean no harm but they have no qualms about picking up your children and handing them around which can be disconcerting for the child and parents. You can feel free to say no to pictures or tell people to stop if it bothers you. If you're looking for more specifically child-friendly activities consider the following:

Parks
Most parks have playgrounds for children. Try Jilani, Lawrence Gardens, or Model Town. While these can tend to get crowded on weekend all of the parks mentioned in the activities section will have areas for children to play and lots of green space for a picnic, Frisbee, football, cricket, or badminton.

Oasis Resort & Water Park
theoasis.com.pk
About an hour's drive from Lahore is Oasis Resort which has a number of activities for children including a water park, horse riding, sand duning, go-karting, cycling, boating, and a large play area.

The Lahore Zoo
lahorezoo.com.pk
On Mall road, right across from Lahore's WAPDA building is the Lahore Zoo. Once one of the largest zoos in Asia and believed to be the fourth oldest in the world, it was established in 1872 although earlier collections of animals were present since 1799. While not the most modern of zoos it remains one of the oldest in the world and still boast a huge number of plant, bird and animal life. It is a good outing for children or an afternoon walk.

Last Word Saturday morning readings
facebook.com/TheLastWordbks
Kids aged 4-8 will enjoy Kids' Story Time at the Last Word Bookstore in Gulberg every Saturday at noon.

Lahore Wildlife Park
Lahore Wildlife Park is located south of the city of Lahore in the outskirts approximately a 45 minutes drive from Mall Road. Established in 1982 it is over 242 acres and considered an extension of the Lahore Zoo. Tickets

are purchased on entry and visitors drive through the park in their vehicles seeing the lions and tigers which roam the park.

Peeru's Café and Puppetry Museum
facebook.com/Peerus.Cafe
Peeru's Café is more well known for its food and live performances of Sufi and Ghazal music than its puppet museum, but tucked behind the open courtyard Peeru's keeps Punjab's puppetry heritage alive with a puppet museum and auditorium.

Joyland
joyland.com.pk
Right outside of Fortress Stadium is an amusement park popular with local families. There are different carnival-like rides and video games available.

Sozo Water Park
sozowaterpark.pk
Out near Jallo Park is Sozo Water Park where you can escape Lahore's hotter months and play all day for 200 PKR per child. 25 acres of water slides, pools, and other fun for the family. Water is filtered with a filtration system and life guards are on duty.

Kids Club Lahore
kidsclub.pk

Depending on how long you're in Lahore you might want to consider signing your kids up for Kids Club which has a huge number of different courses, activities and classes including sports, reading, music and arts, camps and other adventures for kids.

Wonder World
wonderworldsoftplaypakistan.com
When the weather turns hot and you need somewhere to go with kids indoors, Wonder World offers an 'indoor adventure center' for kids right in Gulberg. They have different rooms with play areas, ball pits, slides, climbing walls, and a racing track as well as characters who visit with children and rooms to rent for parties. Gloria Jeans provides the coffee for grown-ups.

The Empty Space Imaginarium
facebook.com/TheEmptySpaceLahore
Right next to Qadaffi Stadium is a new community space where classes are offered for both children and adults. The schedule is normally posted on the facebook page and includes yoga, acting, writing, singing and dancing.

Birdwatching & Bird Circles

Look up at just about any time of day in Lahore and you will see a huge number of birds circling and swooping. The birds are called kites and are common in Eurasia. As scavengers, they glide and fly on air currents searching for food, or prey, and live off meat left for them on the rooftops by residents, small rodents, or trash in the city. They are well adapted to live in cities and have no natural predators, which makes them unafraid of humans. Occasionally, they can be aggressive when swooping for food or protecting their nests but generally are left alone to circle the city.

In addition to the kites there are a number of other birds in Lahore and bird lovers have the best chance of seeing them at either public parks throughout the city or in Changa Manga

forest. In 1965, a study was conducted which estimated there were 240 bird species in the city but another in 1992 found only 101. Some birds are year round residents but some come for only the winter or summer. These include the Indian grey hornbill, yellow-footed green pigeon (easily spotted in Jinnah Gardens), parakeets, doves, the spotted owlet, Old world babblers and flycatchers, mynas, woodpeckers, crows, ashy prinia, redstarts, the red-wattled lapwing, king fishers, and the Oriental white-eye. Winter birds come from the north and migrate in search of food including the yellow-browed warbler, common starling, white wagtail, yellow wagtail, and whit-browed wagtail. Summer birds migrate from the south and also come in search of food and for breeding including the Asian koel, purple sunbird, golden oriole, and cuckoos.

DAY TRIPS
Expand your horizons

Traveling to Other Cities

Daewoo Bus Terminal
daewoo.com.pk
The Daewoo bus is a comfortable and easy way to get between Islamabad and Lahore but also between Lahore and other cities. To book, call the Daewoo Hotline + 92 (0) 331 100 7008 and tell them the date and approximate time you are going from/to. They make a reservation for you and send you a text confirming. You can also check the timings on the website. There are normal buses and super deluxe buses and both are reasonable. In both types of buses there is an attendant who distributes snacks and water and they show a Bollywood movie while you travel.

Daewoo buses run from the central terminal in Lahore. A taxi driver should know where that is. You need to be there 30 minutes early to pick up your reserved ticket. Then, you board the bus and four hours later you are in Rawalpindi. There is no Daewoo station in Islamabad but the station in 'Pindi is close to the motorway and you can hire a Daewoo-taxi to take you to Islamabad for about 1,000 PKR, or there is also a Daewoo shuttle bus to G6. Daewoo is careful about women travelling alone. At all stations they have an extra counter and extra seating areas for women and they normally make sure that women are seated next to other women or behind the bus driver with the attendant.

Q-Connect
qconnect.pk
A new, luxury bus service has just been introduced travelling between Lahore and Islamabad. The Q-Connect service boast luxury coach travel on Volvo buses between the cities. The terminal is, unfortunately, in Cantt near Fortress Stadium which means it is difficult for foreigners to access. However, to book, call +92 (0) 335 777 7777.

Air Travel
www.piac.com.pk
www.airblue.com
www.shaheenair.com
PIA, Air Blue, and Shaheen Airways have flights between most of the major cities in Pakistan. These flights are very affordable often only costing $100 USD a round-trip between Lahore and Islamabad. Be aware, however, that the routes and timings are frequent to change and flights are often delayed or cancelled without good communication to passengers or any compensation.

imply known locally as the 'GT Road' this
one of Asia's oldest and longest roads.
was originally conceived by Afghan
mperor Sher Shah Suri in the 16th century
s a way of expanding and consolidating
is rule, the road stretches from Dhaka to
abul and Lahore falls directly on its path.
n modern-day Pakistan, the GT road runs
rom the Wagah border crossing with India
p to the Torkham border crossing in the
hyber Pass with Afghanistan.

he road is described in countless books
nd histories on South Asia. Anna Suvorova
uotes Rudyard Kipling saying: *"And truly
he Grand Trunk Road is a wonderful
pectacle. It runs straight, bearing without
rowding India's traffic for fifteen hundred
iles—such a river of life as nowhere
lse exists in the world. They looked at
he green-arched, shade-flecked length of
, the white breadth speckled with slow-
acing folk."*

he GT road may be easily taken from
ahore to Islamabad where a visitor will get
 better sense of Pakistan than by travelling
etween the two cities on the motorway.

he food of the GT road is another draw
or visitors. A great cookbook, by Anirudh
.rora and Hardeep Singh Kohli, has been
vritten about the food on the Indian side
f the border but, suffice it to say, the
aste does not stop there. The food on the
Pakistani side is equally as interesting and
elicious.

s you move farther from the border the
ich, heavy curries of Punjab begin to give
vay to the dry, meat BBQ's of the Pashtun
n Khyber Paktunkhwa, which runs from
orthern Pakistan to Afghanistan. Along the
oad you'll find hundreds, if not thousands,
f dhabas (small road side restaurants)
nd truck stops. Many have been there
or generations and have perfected most
of the foods they serve. It is freshly cooked,
he turnover fast, and the clientele (truck
drivers and their assistants) extremely
discerning so if you have the opportunity
o stop for lunch it will be some of the best
Pakistani food you've ever had!

the first Guru and founder of Sikhism, Guru Nanak Dev, was born in
e outside of Sheikhupura. The district has a number of well known Gu
worship). While best known for the famous Hiran Minar (described c
other historical sites worth visiting. The first is the Sheikhupura Qila
, which has an abandoned grandeur with frescoes and mosaics still
Waris Shah, one of Punjab's most famous Sufi poets who lived in the
ther along the Janiala road and many people visit to pay homage.

Changa Manga

Named after a pair of brothers who robbed passers-by and used the forest for a hideout, Changa Manga is located about 80km southwest of Lahore. It used to be the largest man-made, hand planted forest in the world covering approximately 12,000 acres, and was originally planted in 1886 in order to provide timber for the railway. It is now one of three wildlife preserves within the Lahore Division and is only about half its original size, but still has a huge forest area and a conservation and breeding centre for Asiatic vultures. There are a number of walking trails and picnics areas, as well as a 3-mile train which winds through the forest.

Hiran Minar

About an hour's drive west of Lahore along the N60 or the M2 is the town of Sheikhupura. The town is named after Emperor Jahangir who, as a child, was called Sheikhu. The area used to be a hunting ground for the Mughal imperial family. Jahangir, who loved hunting, had a minar (minaret) built in 1606 in memory of his favourite pet antelope, hence the name, Hiran Minar or Minaret of the Antelope. Nearby, Shah Jahan would later build a large complex including a large water tank with sloped sides so animals could come and drink, and an octagonal storeyed pavilion in the centre of the pool. It is a peaceful and picturesque place.

Chiniot

Located just under 2.5 hours to the northwest of Lahore, Chiniot was an important city in the ancient world being occupied by Alexander the Great in 326 BC. It is well known for its beautiful architecture and intricate woodworking. It is thought that carpenters from Chiniot helped carve the woodwork in both the Taj Mahal and the Golden Temple. Wazir Khan, who built the famous mosque in the Old City also hails from Chiniot.

There are a number of beautiful sites to visit, some of which rival those that can be found in Lahore. The Umer Hayat Palace, often called the Taj Mahal of Chiniot, is perhaps the best known, and was built by a trader for his son. The famous shrine of Hazrat Sheikh Ismail Bukhari is also here. Bukhari was a saint who travelled the sub-continent spreading Islam. A sheesh mahal (mirrored palace), which is another shrine, is right next to this one. If you're looking for Mughal architecture, you should also visit the Shahi Masjid. This mosque was built during reign of Shah Jahan and displays intricate wood

carving and artwork. One of the largest remaining Hindu temples in Pakistan which was built around 1848 is in Chiniot.

Rohtas Fort

In the 1500's, Afghan king Sher Shah Suri built an enormous garrison fort to attempt to subdue the local tribes who remained loyal to Mughal emperor Humayun, father of Akbar. Humayun eventually captured the fort and successive empires have used it to rule the region since. Located approximately four hours from Lahore along the Grand Trunk road the fort is situated on a hill about 300 meters above the surrounding areas which gives it some superb views of the Punjab plains. The fort is 4km in circumference, and the outer wall is between 10 and 18 meters thick and constructed of sandstone and brick. The fort could supposedly house up to 30,000 men. Declared a World Heritage Site by UNESCO, there are 12 gates and most are in good repair. It's possible to walk around the entire fort, and there remain a number of sites which should be visited including the museum, the deep step well, and a mosque.

Harappa

Approximately 3.5 hours to the southwest of Lahore along the Lahore-Multan road lies the remains of one of the oldest known civilisations in the world. Harappa (just past the town of Sahiwal) was a city along the Indus that dates back to 2600 BC. In the 1920s, a city of the Harappan civilisation era was discovered near Larkana (in Sindh) called Mohenjo-daro. Harappa was discovered shortly thereafter. The site was badly damaged in the mid-1800s when workers on the Lahore-Multan railway began bringing bricks to the construction saying they had 'discovered' a mine of bricks. As it turned out, bricks do not naturally occur in nature and they were dismantling Harappa.

Tilla Jogian

Tilla Jogian means 'Hill of the Saints' in Punjabi and is the highest peak in the Salt Range, which extends along the Jhelum river between the motorway and the Grand Trunk road. Tilla Jogian is approximately 3,200 feet high and is a sacred place for Hindus, being the point where the sunrise may first be seen. There are the remains of a Hindu monastery there. Sikhs also revere the site, as the founder of Sikhism Guru Nanak spent 40 days in seclusion there.

The Salt Range

Approximately three hours from Lahore on the Lahore-Islamabad motorway is a range of mountains referred to as 'the Salt Range' due to the amount of rock salt found in the hills and the number of salt mines now located there. This is where the world's supply of pink Himalayan salt comes from. There are a few places of interest to visit within the salt range.

Kallar Kahar

A small, tranquil, resort-like town, Kallar Kahar sits on the edge of a natural salt water lake. The town is mainly known for the surrounding sites but is a good place to stop for lunch.

Ketas Temples

Katasraj (or Ketas) is a Hindu temple built for the god Shiva, built around 300 years ago but venerated for much longer. According to legend, when Shiva's wife Parvati died, his tears created two holy ponds—one in Pushkar near Ajmer in India and one in Ketas. The site contains seven temples, a Buddhist stupa, bathhouses and rest houses around the sacred pool. Hindus lived here until Partition when they abandoned the site and migrated to India. Today, Hindus still make a pilgrimage to the site to wash in the pond, believing it contains Shiva's tears and will help attain forgiveness and salvation.

Khewra Salt Mines

These salt mines are the oldest and largest in Pakistan and the second largest in the world. The legend surrounding its origins is that when Alexander the Great was passing through, his troop's horses began licking the ground whereupon it was discovered that the hills contained vast quantities of salt. Today, approximately 350,000 tonnes of the distinctive pink salt are produced each year. The mines are open for visitors and there are a number of tunnels, different sculptures and carvings made entirely out of salt. Visitors can buy lamps and other salt souvenirs.

LAHORE ITINERARIES

Making the most of your time

Answering the question of what you should do and where you should go in Lahore is like answering, 'how long is a piece of string'? There are so many things to do, places to see and food to be eaten that the answer depends on how much time you have. Below you'll find a couple of itineraries that you can use to maximise the time you have but you should feel free to mix and match to suit your tastes and interests.

If you have one full day...

Morning:
- Lahore is not an early rising city so start your day with a proper Lahori breakfast either at your hotel (see box on what should be on the menu) or in the Old City.
- Head to the Delhi Gate and walk into the Old City stopping at the Shahi Hamam and then going to visit Wazir Khan mosque
- Drive around to the entrance of the Fort and spend an hour or two there. Make sure to take a peek over the walls at the Minar-e-Pakistan.
- Walk around to the Hazuri Bagh and Baradari and visit Iqbal's tomb.
- Climb the steps and go see Badshahi mosque.

Lunch:
- If you're not still full from breakfast, have a light lunch at The Delicatessen or The Pantry in Gulberg

Afternoon:
- It's your choice: either get some shopping in along M.M. Alam Road and Liberty Market, OR go tour down Mall Road and visit the Lahore Museum.
- After that, either take a walk around Lawrence Garden on Mall Road.

Dinner:
- If you're in tourist mode head back to the Heera Mandi Food Street in the Old City and eat at Haveli, Cooco's Den, or Andaaz.
- If you're feeling like something special make a reservation at Scafa.

If you have a couple of evenings after work...

You're busy and important, we get that. Your trip is also probably being financed by someone who expects you work all day so you're going to have to prioritise. Here are two evenings out:

Evening #1
After work (but hopefully before sundown) head to the Old City and take in the Lahore Fort and Badshahi Mosque. After that wander over to Heera Mandi food street for Pakistani food overlooking Badshahi.

Evening #2
Tonight is your shopping evening. So you'll first want to check out the different stores/options available. Definitely hit M.M. Alam and Liberty Market in Gulber. For dinner, you'll want to pick from one of the many places in Gulberg depending on the type of food in which you're interested. If you want to stick with Pakistani definitely try Spice Bazaar, or Desi (X2).

If you have a weekend...

Saturday Morning:
◆ Lahore is not an early rising city so start your day with a proper Lahori breakfast either at your hotel (see box on what should be on the menu), at Gawalmandi, Laksmi Chowk, or in the Old City.
◆ Head to the Delhi Gate and walk into the Old City stopping at the Shahi Hamam and then going to visit Wazir Khan mosque
◆ Take a tuktuk through the Old City to Naqsh School for the Arts and tour their gallery
◆ Walk down the street to the Fakir Khana Museum (book this in advance or it might not be open)
◆ Drive to the entrance of the Fort and spend an hour or two there.
◆ Walk around to the Hazuri Bagh and Baradari and visit Iqbal's tomb.
◆ Climb the steps and go see the Badshahi mosque.

Saturday Afternoon:
◆ Grab a snack in the Old City as you're heading to Jahangir's Tomb across the River Ravi and will spend several hours there.
◆ Coming back to Lahore you can stop at Shalimar Gardens if you have time
◆ Drive out to the Wagah Border Ceremony

Saturday Dinner:
◆ Head back to the Heera Mandi Food Street in the Old City and eat at Haveli, Cooco's Den, or Andaaz.

Saturday Night:
◆ Not tired and want to experience the late night life of Lahore? Head to Liberty Market and wander around until the wee hours shopping and people watching.

Sunday Morning:
◆ Have a continental breakfast at the English Tea House, or Coffee and Tea Company, or the Café Upstairs.
◆ Take a tour down Mall Road – on Sunday morning it's virtually empty and you can even walk the length of it (takes about 1 hour from Canal Bank Road to Lower Mall Road).
◆ Stop off at Lawrence Gardens and have a walk around the walking path.
◆ Stop off at the Lahore Museum.

Sunday Afternoon:
◆ Time to do some shopping – head to Gulberg and M.M. Alam

Sunday Dinner:
◆ If you want to see and be seen on the Lahore social scene, reserve a table at Café Aylanto, Lahore Social, or X2.

"'And just like that you look up from your book and you are crossing the Ravi. The sun is calling it a day and heading toward the horizon. The flat plains of Punjab give way to the brick slums. The tents of refuse collectors. Water buffalos in the mud. A white turbaned man stands waist-deep in a green field. People nap under the overpass. Cars race to get home for iftar. The web of electric lines still gathered in the arms of aged electric poles above the streets and canals. A single, illicit kite flown by an anonymous child on a rooftop. The motorway signs beckon you to stay with the promise of Multan. But why? You have reached Lahore and are home."'

- The Author
June 2016

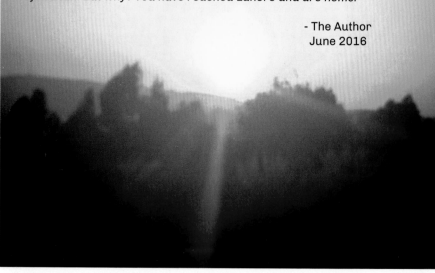